D1467562

Financial Deregulation

The David Hume Institute wishes to thank
Murray Johnstone, Investment Managers
for their generous financial assistance.

Financial Deregulation

The proceedings of a conference held by
The David Hume Institute in May 1986

Edited by Richard Dale

Professor of International Banking and Financial Studies, Heriot-Watt University

Woodhead–Faulkner · Cambridge

Published by Woodhead–Faulkner Ltd
Fitzwilliam House, 32 Trumpington Street,
Cambridge CB2 1QY, England
and
27 South Main Street, Wolfeboro,
New Hampshire, 03894-2069, USA

First Published 1986
© The David Hume Institute 1986

British Library Cataloguing in Publication Data
Financial deregulation: the proceedings of a
    conference held by the David Hume Institute
    in May 1986.
    1. Finance—Great Britain
    I. Dale, Richard   II. David Hume Institute
    322'.0941   HG186.G7

ISBN 0-85941-366-7

Designed by Geoff Green
Typeset by Hands Fotoset, Leicester
Printed in Great Britain by St Edmundsbury Press, Bury St Edmunds, Suffolk

Contents

Foreword   vii

Introduction   ix

1. The regularities of regulation   1
   Professor George Stigler, Nobel Laureate in Economics
   and President of David Hume Institute

2. Financial deregulation: the opportunities and some
   of the dangers   13
   Andrew Buxton, Chairman of Barclays Merchant Bank and
   Vice-Chairman, Barclays Bank PLC

3. The Securities and Investments Board: its objectives
   and expectations   18
   Sir Kenneth Berrill, Chairman, the Securities and
   Investments Board

4. Preparing for the Big Bang   22
   Philip Wilkinson, Group Chief Executive, National
   Westminster Bank PLC

5. A supervisor's perspective on deregulation   28
   Rodney Galpin, Executive Director, Bank of England

6. The audit role in the context of financial deregulation   36
   John Bullock, Senior Partner, Deloitte, Haskins and Sells

7. A review of the legal problems   48
    Professor R. B. Jack, Professor of Mercantile Law, University
    of Glasgow and a Partner, McGricor, Donald and Moncrieff

8. The American experience: bank supervision in the
    United States   64
    L. William Seidman, Chairman, Federal Deposit Insurance
    Corporation, Washington DC

Panel discussion   81

Foreword

The David Hume Institute was established as a company limited by guarantee in January 1985 and is a charity recognized by the Inland Revenue. All the officials give their services free, but the day will soon come when the Institute will have to employ administrative and research staff as a result of the growing demand for its services.

The objects of the Institute are to promote discourse and research on the economic and legal aspects of public policy questions. Initially, the field of government regulation of the economy has been chosen as its major but not exclusive concern. The Institute considers but does not confine itself to Scottish problems. It does approach its subject, however, with a Scottish cast of thought which is derived from David Hume and other major figures of the Scottish Enlightenment.

The Institute has already published, *inter alia*, three studies on regulatory questions of contemporary importance – the regulation of banking, the regulation of women's wages, the EEC regulation of fishing. It sponsored a conference in May 1985 on the reform of pensions which also covered regulatory aspects of the move towards personal pensions. The move towards financial deregulation in 1986 offered the Institute a unique opportunity to draw upon its considerable expertise in this area, and particularly that of Professor Richard Dale, lately of Rothschild's in the City, and now Professor of International Banking and Financial Studies at Heriot-Watt University. The Institute is particularly grateful to him for the professional and editorial arrangements associated with the May 1986 Conference on financial deregulation whose proceedings are found in this volume.

Two happy coincidences made it possible for the Institute to derive further professional support from outside sources. It entered into 'co-production' of the conference with the well-known firm of Deloitte, Haskins and Sells whose advice on production and marketing has contributed to a significant extent to the success of the conference itself. Secondly, it so happened that the Honorary President of the Institute for the period 1984–87, Professor George Stigler, Nobel Laureate in Economics, is a world-famous authority on the economics of regulation in general and financial regulation in particular. He undertook the long journey from Chicago, at some inconvenience during a very busy schedule, in order to deliver a most stimulating address which readers can now savour for themselves.

I have singled out for mention only those aspects of the conference which illustrate how the Institute operates and how it hopes to continue to operate. It goes without saying that the Institute has been particularly fortunate in attracting both outstanding speakers who have provided expert addresses which can now be read by the world at large and an audience of *cognoscenti* in the financial world in Scotland and elsewhere clearly stimulated by what they heard. Judging by their reactions and that of the national financial press, the Institute and Deloitte, Haskins and Sells can fairly claim to have added a useful and important dimension to what is going to be a fascinating debate in the field of public policy.

Alan Peacock
Executive Director

Introduction

Since the late 1970s financial markets world-wide have been character-ised by progressive deregulation. This has involved the removal of barriers to competition both within and between national financial systems and the emergence of global markets in currencies, money market paper, capital market instruments and even equities. Develop-ments now taking place in London, in particular the restructuring of The Stock Exchange and the merging of banking and securities business within financial conglomerates, have to be viewed in this broader context. For it is no longer possible for one financial centre to ignore developments taking place elsewhere. Indeed, if the dismantling of regulatory barriers continues it may soon become difficult to identify distinctive national segments of the global financial marketplace or to separate domestic from 'euro' markets.

Financial deregulation is the result of a wide range of national initia-tives designed to promote the efficiency of domestic capital markets and to attract international financial business. These initiatives can be classified according to whether they are aimed at the liberalisation of international capital movements, the opening up of domestic markets to foreign financial institutions, the removal of constraints on financial diversification, the strengthening of price competition, or the author-isation of innovative financing techniques.

So far as international capital movements are concerned, the most important deregulation move has been the lifting of foreign exchange controls, notably by the UK and Japan in 1979–80. In addition, the removal of tax disincentives to international portfolio investment has played a part, the most significant development here being the abolition of withholding tax during 1984 in the US, Germany and France. Finally, the progressive removal of restrictions on the domestic and Euro-yen bond markets by the Japanese authorities has, since 1984, promoted capital flows into and out of Tokyo.

The extraordinary growth of international capital flows has been accompanied by rapid inter-penetration of national financial markets by foreign institutions seeking to service this business from financial centres covering the major time zones. This 'multinationalisation' of the financial services industry has been encouraged by the relaxation of controls on the entry of foreign banks (for instance in Canada and Australia), by fiscal concessions to offshore financial business and, most recently, by reciprocity deals involving increased representation for Western financial institutions in Tokyo.

The diversification of banks into non-bank financial services is another feature of the deregulation process. Even in those countries (notably the US, Canada and Japan) which prohibit the mixing of banking and securities business banks have been testing the limits of and in some cases finding ways round the law. In London the opening up of Stock Exchange membership to outsiders has led to the formation of a number of financial conglomerates which will undertake banking, corporate advice, issuing, market-making and fund management within the same organisation. The clear trend, therefore, is away from institutional specialisation.

Constraints on price competition are also being removed. In the US the interest ceiling on bank deposits ('Regulation Q') has been phased out, in the UK fixed commissions on stock exchange business are to be abolished while in Japan extensive controls on money market interest rates are being dismantled. More generally, protective pricing arrangements within national markets are being eroded by the intensity of competition between previously discrete sectors of the financial services industry. Indeed, increasingly aggressive price competition has already led to accusations of 'dumping' by financial institutions in some countries.

Finally, financial markets world-wide have been experiencing an extraordinary spate of financial innovation. Partly, this is in response to specific deregulatory actions. For instance several European countries, including the UK, have recently authorised the establishment of domestic markets in commercial paper. And in West Germany, certain financial instruments, such as zero coupon bonds and floating rate notes, were authorised for the first time in 1985. On the other hand, the success of some novel financing techniques, such as revolving underwriting facilities (RUFs) may be due in part to attempts to by-pass existing regulatory constraints in the form of capital adequacy requirements.

What are we to make of the emergence of a global financial services industry largely liberated from geographic, product and pricing constraints? The obvious answer is that users of financial services should benefit from greater efficiency, lower costs and a wider choice of financing and investment possibilities. Some observers, have, however, questioned the desirability of present trends, underlining the increased potential for conflicts of interest and financial instability. For instance, Mr Gerald Corrigan, President of the Federal Reserve Bank of New York, has commented as follows on recent developments in financial markets:

> When we pull together these various elements one message emerges rather powerfully: namely, that events have undercut the effectiveness of many elements of the supervisory and regulatory apparatus historically surrounding banking and finance. If it can't be done onshore, it's done offshore; if it can't be done on the balance sheet, it's done off the balance sheet; and if it can't be done with a traditional instrument, it's done with a new one . . . we must recognise that the historic regulatory/supervisory apparatus associated with banking – whatever its limitations – was a source of restraint and discipline on individual institutions and on the system as a whole. If, therefore, I am correct in postulating that events are undermining that source of restraint, a key question that arises is what, if anything, should replace it?[1]

Paradoxically, therefore, the trend towards financial deregulation and greater competitive freedom has prompted governments and supervisory authorities to review their arrangements for regulating the financial services industry. This review has been most far reaching in the UK where the transformation of financial markets is occurring most rapidly, but a parallel reassessment of regulatory needs is taking place in all the major financial centres. Among the major issues raised are the appropriate objectives of regulation, the machinery of regulation, whether regulation should be directed at financial activities or types of financial institution, the related question of how financial conglomerates should fit into the regulatory framework and, finally, the need for international co-ordination of regulation.

The most widely accepted aims of financial regulation are to limit abuses arising from conflicts of interest and to protect investors and depositors against losses due to the insolvency of financial institutions. In addition, fraud, incompetence, anti-competitive practices and exploitation of investor ignorance are common targets of regulatory action. Conflicts of interest present particularly difficult policy problems. Stringent rules in this area may hamper the smooth operation of financial markets while for mobile markets such as that in Eurobonds the effect may be to drive business into the arms of more accommodating financial centres.

Regulations aimed at protecting the investor against losses generally rely on capital adequacy requirements to reduce the risk of business failure and on compensation schemes to cover investor losses. However, solvency regulation has to cover *all* areas of risk-taking to be effective: a narrow approach based solely on capital adequacy requirements would merely invite the substitution of unregulated for regulated risk. Furthermore, as experience with deposit insurance has shown, protecting the investor against losses through compensation schemes can undermine financial discipline.

The machinery of regulation is another contentious issue. The two main questions here are, firstly, whether the emphasis should be on statutory or self-regulation and, secondly, whether there should be a single all-embracing regulatory authority or a proliferation of such bodies specialising in the regulation of particular types of financial institution or activity.

Policy makers also have to decide whether regulation should be on a 'functional' or an 'institutional' basis. Under a functional approach a given activity would be subject to the same supervisory regime regardless of the type of financial institution undertaking the activity. While such an approach would ensure a truly 'level playing field' for all market participants – the proclaimed goal of most regulators – it would probably require different market activities to be undertaken through separate affiliates within a conglomerate group.

The regulation of financial conglomerates presents formidable difficulties. In the area of solvency or 'prudential' regulation it is crucial to know whether different parts of such an organisation are to be mutually supporting, in the sense that if one part of the business gets into difficulties any liquidity or capital shortfall will be made good by the parent or another affiliate; or whether risks are to be segregated so that the whole group need not be threatened by problems arising in one part of the business. Whether risks are to be pooled or segregated depends on complex questions relating to the commercial and legal interdependence of affiliated businesses. What is clear is that regulatory authorities are only just beginning to confront this problem.

Finally there is the matter of international co-ordination of regulatory policies. With the emergence of global financial markets uneven regulatory practices may have the effect of channelling business to the least regulated centres. In the banking field this danger has been mitigated by the activities of the Cooke Committee, but there is as yet no equivalent mechanism for co-ordinating regulation of securities business.

The papers brought together in this volume cover both sides of the regulation issue: namely, the business opportunities presented by the dismantling of competitive barriers and the need for new regulatory initiatives to deal with the accompanying risks.

Professor Stigler's paper places the debate on financial deregulation in a broader historical and political context, while developing the theory that the extent of state regulation is determined by changes in economic circumstances rather than by shifts in ideology. Mr Buxton focuses on the economic benefits of deregulation from the viewpoint of both the new financial conglomerates and the end-users of financial services. Sir Kenneth Berrill deals with the development of London's new self-regulatory bodies under the Securities and Investments Board. The preparations by National Westminster Bank for London's Big Bang are the subject of Mr Wilkinson's comments – which include the chilling forecast that in five years' time there will be only ten major players in the UK securities markets, commanding 60 to 70 per cent of the total business.

Speaking as a leading regulator, Mr Galpin then identifies some of the risks facing London's deregulated financial markets while also pointing to the twin dangers of overlap and underlap in the supervision of bank conglomerates. From a vantage point somewhere between that of the regulator on the one hand and the market practitioner on the other, Mr Bullock discusses how far auditors can be part of the regulatory process in a situation where the interest of customers or depositors may differ from those of shareholders. Professor Jack gives us a legal assessment of a number of problems arising out of the UK's new regulatory arrangements, including the potential for cross-infection within financial conglomerates, the emergence of new conflicts of interest following the abandonment of the 'single capacity' distinction between brokers and jobbers, and the difficulties of applying a 'fit and proper' test to those carrying on investment business.

Finally, Mr Seidman provides a transatlantic perspective based on recent US experience with a deposit insurance system that has helped to stabilise the banking system in the United States – at the cost of removing market penalties for excessive risk-taking.

Richard Dale
Heriot-Watt University
May 1986

1 Remarks before the New York State Bankers' Association on 30 January 1986.

1 The regularities of regulation

Professor George Stigler
Nobel Laureate and President of David Hume Institute

In this key opening section Professor Stigler develops the theory that the extent of state regulation is determined less by shifts in ideology than by changing economic circumstances. When applied to the deregulation of US financial markets this theory suggests that the abandonment of interest rate ceilings, the abolition of minimum commissions and, most recently, the first tentative moves towards interstate banking, represent responses to economic pressures rather than a revulsion against public regulation. No doubt this theory would fit equally well in the UK context where the changing shape of financial markets appears to be dictating regulatory developments rather than vice versa.

The share of economic life under the control of government has undergone an enormous expansion in the past 100 years. The share of the nation's income that has been spent by governments has risen perhaps three- to five-fold in the western world during this period. The share of the labour force directly employed by governments has experienced a similar expansion. No simple, satisfactory measure can be assigned to governmental regulations of economic life at any time, but the inundation of the economy by present-day regulations must, in comparison to the past, be as Noah's flood was to a normal spring. Is deregulation the Ark on which private enterprise will reach its former domain? This is the question I shall attempt to answer.

Explanations for state action

Two main types of explanation have been given for social movements as widespread, as persistent and as powerful as the expansion of the economic functions of the modern state. The first attributes this magnitude of development to a massive change in the opinions of people, the second attributes this development to the changing circumstances of society.

Opinion and public policy

I take as a most important proponent of the view that opinion rules governments and men, Albert Venn Dicey, whose *Law and Public Opinion in England* is a classical exposition of the view. He would not claim originality; on the contrary, he would claim much ancient authority for the position that there exists a 'close dependence of legislation . . . upon the varying currents of public opinion'.[1] He carved the nineteenth century into three periods:

1   The Period of Legislative Quiescence (1800–1830)
2   The Period of Benthamism or Individualism (1825–1870)
3   The Period of Collectivism (1870–1900)

Throughout the century there was a 'close and immediate connection . . . between public opinion and legislation'.[2] Dicey did not assert such a relationship to be characteristic of all societies: primarily in England, and primarily after 1800, it was the opinion of those who take 'an effective part in political life' that dictated public policy.[3]

Dicey could have cited among his ancient authorities David Hume, who assigned primacy of influence to opinion, even ignorant opinion. His magnificent essays made immense advances in the theory of money and trade, but observe their stance. He is consistently seeking to eliminate the intellectual confusion to which he attributes the unsocial policies of Europe. Thus the essay *The Balance of Trade* begins:

> It is very usual, in nations ignorant of the nature of commerce, to prohibit the exportation of commodities, and to preserve among themselves whatever they think valuable and useful.

His close friend, Adam Smith, paid more attention to the sinister interests of the parties who benefited from such policies, but also leaned heavily upon ignorant opinion as an explanation for public policies.

The assignment of a high influence to opinion and its makers did not stop with Dicey. I need hardly cite the famous peroration with which Keynes closed the *General Theory*: '. . . the ideas of economists and political philosophers, both when they are right and when they are wrong, are more powerful than is commonly understood. Indeed the world is ruled by little else.' Milton Friedman is more explicit:

The example of India and Japan . . . exemplifies the importance of the intellectual climate of opinion, which determines the unthinking pre-conceptions of most people and their leaders, their conditioned reflexes to one course of action or another.

The Meiji leaders who took charge of Japan in 1867 were dedicated primarily to strengthening the power and glory of their country. They attached no special value to individual freedom or political liberty. They believed in aristocracy and political control by an élite. Yet they adopted a liberal economic policy that led to the widening of opportunities for the masses and, during the early decades, greater personal liberty. The men who took charge in India, on the other hand, were ardently devoted to political freedom, personal liberty and democracy. Their aim was not only national power but also improvement in the economic conditions of the masses. Yet they adopted a collectivist economic policy that hamstrings their people with restrictions and continues to undermine the large measure of individual freedom and political liberty encouraged by the British.

The difference in policies reflects faithfully the different intellectual climates of the two eras. In the mid-nineteenth century it was taken for granted that a modern economy should be organised through free trade and private enterprise. It probably never occurred to the Japanese leaders to follow any other course. It is an interesting sidelight that both views came from Great Britain. The Japanese adopted the policies of Adam Smith. The Indians adopted the policies of Harold Laski.[4]

It is understandable that the two economists of the twentieth century who succeeded in becoming major figures not only in scholarship but also in the very different world of policy discussion should assign a large value to opinion makers.

For ideology to be a useful theory of governmental functions, it is surely necessary to explain how ruling opinion is formed and in response to what forces opinion changes. There are hints of a 'great man' theory of political opinion in Dicey[5] – hence his label of the age of Bentham – which became more definite in Friedman, but such hints are merely illustrative. There were, of course, important leaders of opinion on the side of *laissez-faire* in Dicey's time: Herbert Spencer, William H. Mallock, and Alfred Marshall are examples. One could fill a whole lecture with the pairings of names of strongly divergent advisors on policy today. Great men are made great by representing important movements rather than by creating such movements. So let us turn to our second explanation for the expansion of the economic functions of the state.

The self-interest theory

The self-interest hypothesis assumes that societies consistently behave in the same way with respect to the use of the state at all times. Any group in the society that has access to political influence will use that influence when it can improve its position. The composition of the groups that have access to political influence will depend upon the economic and social structure of the society. The composition and the desired pro-grammes of these groups will depend also upon the society's political institutions, although over longer periods these institutions are surely partially or wholly responsive to the underlying economic and social structure.

In short, the hypothesis is that the propensity to use the state is like the propensity to use coal: we use coal when it is the most efficient resource with which to heat our houses and power our factories. Similarly, we use the state to build our roads or tax our consumers when the state is the most efficient way to reach those goals. At all times men will use the resources they command to best effect: the efficient pursuit of one's interests requires this kind of behaviour, and the requirement is generally fulfilled.

When the conditions of the society dictate little use of the state, the economy will be characterised as *laissez-faire*. When the conditions of the society dictate much use of the state, the economy will be called collec-tivistic or welfare or (better) politicised. To explain why a society moves from one of these regimes to the other, one does not look (primarily) to intellectual currents: rather, the explanation will lie chiefly in the changing scope for governmental action as the structure of the economy changes.

Cannot the state always play a large role in economic life? I think not. For example, in a rural society there is a much smaller possible role for the provision of public services such as education and medical care. Governments much prefer to supply services, which cannot be resold by their recipients, instead of goods. In such a society, income is ill-defined and not a suitable object of taxation, so property becomes the leading basis for taxation. However, it is difficult to tax property progressively because its ownership can often be subdivided. I shall shortly give more examples of how economic and social circumstances influence the possibilities of state action.

I propose to test this hypothesis that circumstances, not ideological preferences with respect to the proper arena of state action, will determine what tasks the state undertakes. I shall make two tests. The first is to examine the reasons for the *laissez-faire* policies in the United States in the first half of the nineteenth century. The second test is an examination of the movement to deregulate the financial markets in America in the past 15 years.

Laissez-faire in nineteenth-century America

Consider the economic conditions in the United States in 1840. In that year four-fifths of the labour force was in agriculture, and except along the Atlantic seaboard from Massachusetts to Maryland, the share was usually closer to nine-tenths. Only one person in 12 lived in a city over 10,000. Much of manufacturing was decentralised for local markets: the largest employer was house construction (then included in manufacturing), and the other major manufacturing industries included flour and saw mills, building materials, printing, carriages and furniture. Textiles was the only large manufacturing industry that was geographically concentrated. It was centred in New England and the middle Atlantic states – and of course it obtained tariff protection.

In a history of economic legislation in Iowa, I.L. Pollock observed the following:

> Throughout its history Iowa has been primarily an agricultural Commonwealth . . . At the same time, an examination of the statute books reveals the fact that in Iowa relatively little legislation has been enacted for the promotion or regulation of agricultural interests.[6]

Is it a paradox that the overwhelmingly important class of a community did not use its power over the state to seek economic advantages by legislation? Not at all; there were few economic advantages to be procured by this route: the determinants of the prosperity of Iowa agriculture were not within the jurisdiction of the legislature. Iowa farmers could not use their legislature to increase the prices of their main products, which were set in national or world markets: Liverpool was well beyond the reach of either Iowa or the federal government. Farmers could not find enough non-farmers to obtain boons through discriminatory taxation and expenditures.

The main area of economic life in which there was large scope for conferring benefits upon particular groups was in transportation. The rivalry of Baltimore, Philadelphia, New York, and Boston to become the leading entry and export depot for the Midwest is a familiar theme in the literature on internal improvements. The states conferred large positive and negative capital gains upon landowners by their choices of routes of turnpikes, canals, and then railroads. It is regrettable that the economic historians have paid little attention to these efforts of regions within states to achieve large gains and avoid large losses in land values.[7]

It is interesting to note that the economic historians do not cite a general rule of *laissez-faire* as a common or important argument employed in the debates over public policy.[8] When Andrew Jackson vetoed the Maysville Road Bill in 1830, thus withdrawing the federal government from internal improvements for a generation, with a veto message of magisterial turgidity, he rested his case on the constitution, not the doctrine of *laissez-faire*. The historians of English thought are equally emphatic on the absence of doctrinaire *laissez-faire* – in a famous essay, Brebner challenged Dicey to the extent of calling Bentham the patron saint of intervention.[9]

In short, agricultural America was not a good soil on which to plant extensive governmental functions or expenditures, and that circumstance governed governments. I must note that a fuller discussion would force me to face the uncomfortable fact that numerous agricultural nations today have extensive governmental programmes regulating agriculture. As a first approximation I would explain that difference by the absence in these modern societies of effective democracy or freedom of movement.

Deregulation of the financial markets

The past 15 years have been held out as a period of wide-ranging deregulation of the financial markets of the United States. The extent of the deregulation is all the more remarkable because of the length of time some of the regulations have been in place. Consider just a few major steps:

1   The commission rates of the New York Stock Exchange had been fixed by a powerful cartel since 1792, and operated under the protection of the Securities and Exchange Commission after 1934. The minimum rate structure was abolished within the period from 1968 to 1975.

2   The gradual, virtually completed, abolition of the controls over maximum interest rates payable by commercial banks and savings institutions has taken place during the past eight years. These maxima had been in effect for over 40 years.

3   The geographical expansion of banks over state lines was prohibited until recently. Now regional state banking compacts have led to broadening markets.

4   There has been an extensive development of so-called non-banks, that is, banks that do not have both demand deposits and commercial loans. These non-banks can be owned by brokerage houses, insurance companies, and even retailers, since they escape the legal limitations on the range of activities permitted to bank holding companies.

5   The barriers protecting the specialisation of financial institutions have been lowered. Commercial bankers can act as stock brokers and in turn stock brokers can act as banks through their money market accounts.

Has this rapid and sweeping reorganisation of the financial markets been due to a change of opinion? Have the inefficiencies of the previous structure, well documented in a hundred economic studies, and the preachings of Keynes' academic scribblers brought about a renewed appreciation of the free market? I offer the alternative explanation that these policy changes were dictated by the changing economic conditions of the nation.

I shall identify five large changes in the economic environment of the capital markets in the past half-century. Each is of a magnitude essentially unprecedented in the history of American financial markets.

1   Surely the pride of place, or rather the shame of place, has been the inflation, which brought the Consumer Price Index in 1980 to over six times the level of 1940, and in 1985 to four times the level of 1953. Nor were these vast increases achieved by a steady rise of prices: in each of the years 1974, 1979, and 1980, prices rose over 12 per cent – approaching the levels of the pent-up inflation of 1946.

2   As a result of this major inflation, interest rates reached levels previously unrecorded.

   (a)   Three-month Treasury bills yielded 1.2 per cent in 1950 and 16.3 per cent in May of 1981.

   (b)   The rate on long term AAA corporate bonds rose from 2.6 per cent in 1950 to 14.2 per cent in 1981.

Correspondingly, the real rate of interest was negative from 1973 through 1980.

3   Pension fund and insurance company investments in common stocks grew at a rate that taxes one's vocabulary. In 1945 these investments were $3 billion, in 1970, $96 billion, and in 1983, $452 billion. This is an annual rate of increase of 14.1 per cent. For reference, Malthus expressed fear at the potentialities of a population growth of 2.8 per cent per year.

4   Largely because of the growth of institutional stock holdings, institutional trading on the New York Stock Exchange rose from 30 per cent of all trading in the 1950s to 70 per cent today. Block trades of 10,000 shares or more rose from 3.1 per cent of shares traded in 1965 to 41.0 per cent in 1982. Americans increasingly shifted to intermediaries the task of investing in securities.

5   I surmise that the development of the modern computer, which has revolutionised data processing, has had substantial effects on the financial system. My colleague, Robert Graves, has pointed out

that if the automobile industry had progressed at the same rate as the computer industry in the past 25 years, a Rolls Royce would cost $2.00 and it would get about 100,000 miles to the gallon. The efficiency in multiple uses of data has fostered both large-scale and diversified scope of operations.

These five developments are without precedent in American history.

Let us now examine how these fundamental changes in the environment of the financial markets were related to the acts of deregulation.

1   Prior to 1968 the New York Stock Exchange forbade any quantity discounts for large trades, and set commissions that rose rapidly with the price of the shares traded. The profits on large block transactions were enormous at these rates, and brokers competed for these transactions by supplying elaborate investment analyses. Soon, to accommodate the fact that traders and investment analysts were different groups, the 'give-up' appeared, whereby the trader gave up much of the commission to a broker specialising in investment analysis. The 'third market' (an over-the-counter market) and the institutional memberships of financial enterprises in regional stock exchanges further eroded the New York Stock Exchange's position. The prohibition of the setting of minimum commissions in 1975 merely recognised the impossibility of adhering to unrealistic commission rates.

2   Savings institutions necessarily accumulated large stocks of ageing mortgages during the 1970s, with average interest rates of perhaps 7 per cent, but the interest rates on new mortgages reached 16.7 per cent by 1981. Meanwhile, these same institutions were losing their ability to attract new savings, so that eventually they approached universal insolvency, concealed only by federal assistance. The limitations on the interest rates paid on savings accounts and the saving institutions themselves could not both survive. In many cases neither survived.

3   Similarly, the commercial banks lost their ability to attract or hold deposits under the ceilings on interest rates, forcing the elimination of interest rate ceilings, the authorisation of interest-yielding checking (NOW) accounts, and eventually money market accounts.

4   The sudden termination of a major inflation has proved as painful as the inflation itself. The values of many durable assets, among them agricultural land and several energy resources, collapsed once the price level began to stabilise. The widespread failures of lending institutions followed, calling forth a measure of interstate banking as solvent financial institutions were assisted in taking over insolvent banks and savings institutions.

This terse recital is sufficient, I believe, to justify the claim that the main contours of the recent evolution of the financial markets in the United States can be explained without recourse to a revulsion against public regulation. In explaining why one does not walk from Dover to Calais it should suffice to point to the Channel, without adding that such a long walk would be fatiguing.

Not only do we dispense with an emergent ideology of deregulation to explain the acts of deregulation, but also we cannot fail to observe that much regulation of the financial markets has survived and new regulatory actions continue to be taken. As a tiny instance, after 20 years of hard fighting, the commercial banks are still not allowed to underwrite revenue bonds of state and local governments, although they have long been able to underwrite general obligation bonds. Paul Volker, riding on the glory that comes from financing a major inflation and then its stabilisation, is prepared to have the Federal Reserve System regulate much of the capital markets. The nationalisation of Continental Illinois Bank should be viewed as powerful new regulation.

Moreover, I predict that when the economic environment has stabilised for a time, we shall see new regulations serving to shelter the new financial markets that will develop. Neither the desire of industries to obtain governmental favours nor the willingness of governments to confer such favours on influential industries will have changed.

A role for economists?

I have not concealed my deep scepticism of the role of opinion, and opinion leaders, in bringing about basic changes in direction of a society. Does that leave any important role for the academic scribblers whose influence Keynes assessed so high? I believe it does – in fact as an economist I better had – and in a thoroughly old-fashioned way.

When a scientist discovers something that is new and true, a rational society must accept that finding whether it is benevolent or hateful. A rational person cannot disregard an established finding such as that X is a wonderful antibiotic, Y a lethal poison, and Z a reliable pattern of human behaviour under governmental price-setting. Different people may wish to use a new finding in different ways, but only at one's own peril may it be ignored.

Therefore the truly established findings of economists are incorporated into all economic policies. No one disputes the fundamental law of demand, that buyers will seek to purchase more of a thing when its price is reduced. When a government introduces effective price ceilings without formal rationing, it does not disregard the law of demand; it simply decides that it prefers the pattern of purchases that will result with queuing. I would claim a modest role in the deregulation of the financial markets for the modern theories of efficient markets and of economic regulation.

It follows that the most important economists are those who discover and prove general relationships in economic life. They are vastly more influential in the long run than those other economists who become famous on the stage of public discussion.

This second role of the economist – the formulating of desirable public policy – fills a different and much less influential function.

Whether the circumstances of a society dictate little or extensive use of the state in any area of economic life, it is appropriate to devise philosophies or theories to describe these general practices. When the state makes few interventions in economic affairs, it is natural for this practice to be articulated in a philosophy of *laissez-faire*, and that philosophy is then the first, general reaction to any new proposals for state action. When the state is vigorous and far-ranging in an area (as, for example, is presently true of environmental protection), it is equally natural for new extensions of that programme to be welcomed, and attacks upon it repulsed, by a philosophy of state responsibility.

These philosophies are useful summaries of the general state of contemporary political equilibrium: they provide a first answer to proposed changes in policy that are reasonably good predictors of how the new proposals will fare. If they are widely used, we may be confident that they will not be rigorous and abstract, and therefore they are better named philosophies than theories.

The philosophies are constructed out of actual practices and trends in these practices by spokesmen of the groups that support or oppose the practices. These spokesmen are representatives of the affected groups and include political representatives and that class with the flattering name of 'intellectuals'. The philosophies or ideologies are not simply descriptive of actual (or desired) policies: inevitably they codify and put a measure of consistency in the approved practices and, therefore, exert an influence on what is acceptable.

Consider, for example, the laws passed by Parliament in 1824 to legalise the exportation of machines and the emigration of skilled workers. Probably neither of these attempts to hamper foreign competition was effectively enforceable, but the chief power groups in the British Parliament would not be eager to repeal them. Yet the repeal was in keeping with the general tendency to repeal legislation that was restrictive of free trade, and that policy was a primary goal of the rising industrial classes.

This second role of articulating and preaching the philosophies of important groups in the society is obviously useful, and commands both prestige and income. Nor is it a role that requires a spokesman to support policies that he personally does not wish to be followed: there are many groups among which one can choose. A good measure of integrity of the spokesmen of the various classes is compatible with their earning approximately equal rewards.

Conclusion

The interests of the various groups in a society are durable: there have been identifiable farm blocs, unionised workers, urban poor, manufacturing and other such interests for many years or even many decades. Opinions usually change more rapidly than these economic and social classes. It follows, therefore, that shorter-term changes in public policies may be due to the changeable winds of opinion as well as to the shorter-term changes in economic environments. If I believed that an economist could say much that was useful about the short-run changes in public policy, I would have given more time and especially more thought to opinions.

On this reading of the nature of the fundamental forces in the political process, the scope for reformers is narrowly confined. That should hardly be news to anyone, and especially to economists whose two-century-long efforts to achieve freer international trade have seldom prospered. Yet I find a consoling merit in the dominance of long-run social and economic policy by the social and economic structure of the society. If our nations will not listen closely to the excellent advice economists give, these same nations will be equally deaf to the score of nonsensical and pernicious proposals that spring up with the frequency of general elections. If we cannot have wisdom, perhaps we should be satisfied with predictability.

1 Dicey, A. V. *Law and Public Opinion*, (Macmillan, London, 2nd ed., 1914), p. 1.
2 *Ibid.*, p. 7.
3 *Ibid.*, p. 10.
4 Friedman, M. *Free to Choose* (Harcourt, Brace Jovanovich, 1980), p. 285.
5 In fact Dicey makes a fatal concession to the alternative theory we shall soon present:
   Now it must at once be granted that in matters of legislation men decided in the main by their real or apparent interest. So true is this, that from the inspection of the laws of a country it is often possible to conjecture, and this without much hesitation, what is the class which holds, or has held, predominant power at a given time. [*Ibid.*, pp. 12–13]
   If opinion is the expression of the interests of the effective political participants, why then emphasise opinion instead of interest as the prime mover? Dicey's reply is that interest no doubt plays a powerful role in fixing one's political goals, but that interest is not nakedly revealed (*ibid.*, pp. 14–15).
6 *History of Economic Legislation in Iowa* (State Historical Society, Iowa City, 1918), p. 67. A similar remark is made about coal mining, *ibid.*, p. 81.

7 See for example Goodrich, Carter, *Government Promotion of American Canals and Railroads, 1800–1890* (Columbia University Press, 1960), pp. 8 and 46 and Ch. 3; Goodrich, C., *Canals and American Economic Development* (Columbia University Press, 1961), pp. 69, 129–31, 178, 253 and especially pp. 234–35:

> Between 1820 and 1846 the value of land and improvements, adjusted for changes in the general price level, in the 14 counties bordering the Erie Canal increased by 91 per cent. During the same period the real value of property in the non-canal counties, excluding New York and Kings counties (Manhattan and Brooklyn), increased by only 52 per cent while property values in the state as a whole increased by 66 per cent.

See also J. A. Durrenberger, *Turnpikes* (privately printed, Columbia Dissertation, Valdosta, Ga., 1931), pp. 47, 127.

8 See Handlin, O., 'Laissez-Faire Thought in Massachusetts, 1790–1880', *Journal of Economic History Supplement: The Tasks of Economic History*, III, 1943, pp. 55–56; and *Commonwealth: Massachusetts, 1774–1861* (New York University Press, 1947); Heath, M., 'Laissez-Faire in Georgia, 1732–1860'. *Journal of Economic History Supplement*, 1943, pp. 78–100; *Constructive Liberalism: The Role of the State in the Economic Development of Georgia to 1860* (Harvard University Press, 1954); and Hartz, L., *Economic Policy and Democratic Thought: Pennsylvania, 1776–1860* (Harvard University Press, 1948).

9 Brebner, J. B., 'Laissez-Faire and State Intervention in Nineteenth-Century Britain', in *The Tasks of Economic History* VIII (1948), pp. 59–73. A survey of much of the modern literature is given in a book by Taylor repeating Brebner's title: Taylor, A. J., *Laissez-faire and State Intervention in Nineteenth Century Britain* (Macmillan, London, 1972). See also Scott Gordon, H., 'The Ideology of Laissez-Faire', in *The Classical Economists and Economic Policy*, ed. by Coats, A. W., (Methuen & Co., London, 1971), pp. 180–205, and the interesting essay by Aydelotte, W. D., 'The Conservative and Radical Interpretations of Early Victorian Social Legislation', *Victorian Studies*, December 1967.

2 Financial deregulation: the opportunities and some of the dangers

Andrew Buxton
Vice-Chairman of Barclays Bank PLC

Whereas Professor Stigler is concerned with the theory of deregulation, Andrew Buxton presents a practitioner's view of current developments in the United Kingdom. He underlines the point that the changes sweeping UK financial markets are part of a much wider trend affecting the global financial services industry and that new instruments and financing techniques developed in one market are quickly transplanted to others. But he also provides support to Stigler's theory when he asserts that the deregulation of The London Stock Exchange would have been brought about by external competitive pressures even if there had been no agreement with the government to liberalise the Exchange's rulebook.

My purpose is to discuss financial deregulation in the world, rather than just in the United Kingdom, because it is the world market that is changing and the United Kingdom is only part of it. It is an important part, however, because London has the luck to be in the time zone between Tokyo and New York and so can trade with both on the same day. London also has the advantage of being grouped in the same time zone as lesser but nevertheless important markets, such as Geneva, Frankfurt and Paris.

What do we really mean by deregulation? Some people in the United Kingdom will immediately think of the breaking of The Stock Exchange cartels, but others will think of the granting of new banking licences to Japanese security houses in London, matched of course by similar action by Japanese authorities in allowing British banks to obtain securities licences in Japan – a welcome piece of practical bargaining by the Treasury and the Bank of England. I am sure some would include the relaxing of regulations in Australia which has enabled companies like my own to buy 50 per cent of an Australian stockbroker. Others would include the introduction of new markets, such as the commercial paper market in France or the Netherlands, shortly to be followed by a similar market here in London. It might even be the relaxation of building society restrictions on lending in this country or the spread of the money centre banks in the United States into regional banking centres. I suspect that financial deregulation embraces a wide range of relaxations which have one thing in common: relevant authorities have allowed the market to change its participants or its products. I hope, however, that no one means that the resultant markets or products are unregulated.

These changes have been creeping up on us for a number of years and they have at their heart over-capacity and great competition in financial markets, coupled with the so-called securitisation of debt. Traditional bank lending in the corporate market is increasingly being replaced by the use of tradable securities, as sophisticated and determined corporate treasurers look for the cheapest source of funds and technology permits rapid access to international information and markets. The explosive growth of the swap market has in effect integrated all the financial markets of the world. Traditional constraints on market currency and interest rate structures have now, through swap techniques, been unbundled. A corporation can now seek the cheapest source of debt, theoretically in any market in the world and swap the transaction into the precise currency and interest-rate structure desired. This process has also been encouraged by investors who have shown a liking for the liquid instruments that have been provided and who have been remarkably receptive to the innovative financial structures. Given the shocks in the financial markets in recent times, investors have realised that many corporate credits are now better than bank risks, so they prefer corporate paper in their portfolios to the bank paper they used to hold.

The effects on the New York money centre banks have been dramatic. It is not that their total asset bases have been diminished, but that growth has been slowed. The experience has been varied but generally the largest banks have achieved their growth in the middle corporate market where bank lending remains of a traditional nature and in overseas activities. Certain specialist wholesale banks have, however, realised the implications for their balance sheets and have been prepared to accept slow growth on interest-bearing assets, whilst they have concentrated resources on fee-income generation, through arranging funding, and on trading income, through dealing in debt securities.

New York, of course, is the one leading financial centre in the world where deregulation has largely ground to a halt in the face of the Glass-Steagall Act. A bank which takes retail deposits cannot trade in equity security markets and, as banks move further and further into the securities markets, some of them are publicly wondering whether to give up their retail branch networks in order to trade more widely in the securities markets.

Meanwhile, elsewhere in the world the process of deregulation continues as these new financial methods transfer from one centre to another. A commercial paper market is seen to be a success in New York so it is allowed in Paris. Dollar denominated Floating Rate Notes are commonplace, so we now find that Germany allows Deutschmark FRN and the Netherlands allows guilder FRN.

London has always been a relatively free market which is one of its strengths. It is, therefore, natural for its financial institutions to extend their activities into securities dealing as the world market changes. The deregulation of the London Stock Exchange would have been brought about by external competition pressures if it had not been triggered by the case in the Restrictive Practices court against the Exchange rules, since The Stock Exchange was already seeing some of its business slipping away to better capitalised and better managed foreign firms operating outside the restrictions of The Stock Exchange.

The introduction of powerful partners into under-capitalised stockbrokers and stock jobbers presents an opportunity for them to compete in international markets. In turn it brings to the banks or merchant banks a wider distribution capability and a wider dealing capability than they had before.

In some cases there should be other advantages to the main partners. A large international bank probably has off-shoots overseas (if not in this country) which are already involved in some way in securities trading. Barclays, for instance, in addition to a fund management business in this country, already has among its subsidiaries a stockbroker in Holland, a Stock Exchange seat in Milan and a fund-management business in Switzerland, together with other subsidiaries which impact on securities dealing of some form or another. A strong presence in the domestic centre of its business will pull these international businesses together and will also give an additional international extension to the domestic business.

The moves into the deregulated market by large banks are, therefore, prompted partly by market competition and partly by a desire to add to their already wide services. Are they more likely to benefit the end user of the financial services? In principle the answer should be that the City Revolution will result in a better and cheaper service for the corporate user. Competition has already brought down the price of basic cash banking and it will now bring down the price of securities deals. On the corporate finance side one is already beginning to see signs of the introduction of bought deals in which the investment banker will tell the company raising new capital 'I will buy the whole transaction at an agreed price and will place the paper on the market myself without the need for a plethora of managers, underwriters and sub-underwriters, etc.'. Such an offer could be very attractive to a corporate treasurer who can be assured that his paper can be placed in an orderly manner and at less cost, although the wide-spread use of the bought deal will, to some extent, depend on whether pre-emption rights for shareholders continue. In the retail market, is there any reason why a clearing bank should not run an automated dealing service through its branches or indeed through terminals supplied to the corporate customers at prices which would undercut most stockbrokers? The clearing banks today process a comparatively high percentage of small Stock Exchange orders and they should be able to build on that. In between those extremes the professional investor will be able to choose how much and in what ways he pays for research and other services.

There will still be a place for the specialist, since experience in other markets shows that there is always a market for skill and specialisation. A firm may be skilled at handling private clients, it may specialise and research regional stocks or a particular market sector, and if it provides a good service it will get business from all quarters. The new market will, however, expose the firm which is merely providing an indifferent service at a high price.

Choice apparently improves, therefore, and price, through competition, comes down, which looks good for the end user; but it does mean that the seller of the services will need a strong capital base and a strong skill base in order to make money. There is an obvious risk that a bank is going into the markets which are new territories at a time when competition is at its greatest. That is, of course, one reason why banks have been prepared to pay what look like ridiculous salaries for skills in the new market, because there could be no justification whatsoever for investing in anything other than the best available. One is still left, however, wondering whether all 28 of the potential operators in the gilt market are really going to make money.

The Bank for International Settlements has recently pointed out that the returns in some sectors of the securities market do not justify the risks and that is a fact which financial institutions will do well to make a note of. Many of the risks taken by banks in the securitised debt market are at present off balance sheet, and this has encouraged the lenders or the underwriters to accept lower returns than if capital had been required to back the transaction. It might also mean that some banks have accepted unjustified underwriting risks in their quest for off-balance sheet income. Those who are offered Revolving Underwriting Facilities or Note

Issuance facilities would do well to ask whether all the underwriting banks will be able to produce the facilities when the crunch comes. There is now, of course, a concerted move by central banks to ensure that financial institutions are better capitalised and that the risks are backed by capital, but it is a slow process and depends on the willingness of the individual central banks to tackle their banking sector. The Bank of England has been a leader in this process and rightly so, and the British banks want to see that process energetically pursued in other countries.

The securities markets are volatile and complex. The new markets will depend heavily on computer systems so the management of fast-moving risk is improved. Woe betide any firm which attempts to operate in the new markets without the systems to back it up. They lay themselves open to high risk of business loss and of fraud.

The complexity of the securities markets brings me to the protection of the investor and conflicts of interest, both of which should be subjects near to the heart of every participant in the securities industry. The principles are not new, particularly for a bank which has conflicts of interest between its lending, its corporate advice and its fund management functions. I suspect that most reputable businesses will have their own internal codes of practice and will certainly, for instance, physically separate their fund management and dealing functions, even if that is not required by law. I think this emphasises that ultimately it is the individual firms that an investor must trust to handle his business.

Of course, this trust must be backed by codes of practice and by law, and it is surely in the industry's interest to produce a background which is acceptable to Government with the customers' interest in mind. We must not forget, however, that whatever the background, conflicts of interest will arise every day in an integrated securities business that is dealing, distributing and managing funds. It is up to each firm to manage those functions with integrity. Each firm must, however, realise that the industry as a whole should project that integrity as a public face because an industry's face can be tarnished by cowboys. If we are to encourage the small investor, and he certainly needs encouragement, he must be offered financial security in addition, but I do not think that it should be necessary to protect the financially sophisticated institution. We must be careful not to over legislate. London has every chance of becoming a major securities market provided its entrepreneural skills are allowed to flourish.

I am optimistic that sensible deregulation will benefit us all. There are indeed risks, but they can be managed. Investors, banks, dealers or brokers, will deal with people who are strong enough to manage the risk, and skilful enough to gain the opportunities – that is the future.

3 The Securities and Investment Board: its objectives and expectations

Sir Kenneth Berrill

Chairman of Securities and Investment Board

Moving from the concerns of the market practitioner to those of the regulator, Sir Kenneth Berrill traces the progress of the new regulatory framework that is to govern the UK financial services industry. One particular difficulty is that the new legal structure will not be in place until well after the Big Bang has occurred. Sir Kenneth here warns that financial institutions must anticipate the new regulatory arrangements and that waiting until the last moment would be a dangerous policy.

The objectives of the Securities and Investments Board are to provide a system of effective investor protection across the UK markets and, at the same time, to ensure that those markets develop efficiently and competitively. Achieving only one half of that two-fold aim, whichever half it might be, would be failure.

But our expectations are very much that the overall package can be achieved and that, when the initial dust-storms, aroused by the plans for the new system, have died down, the markets themselves will acknowledge that the United Kingdom is to have a better and a more coherent framework for regulation of investment business than ever before.

The Board has already begun to issue various draft sections of the new rule book, and over the next two months that procedure will be speeded up with tranches of draft rules and consultative documents on subjects including client money regulations, compensation funds and our own authorisation procedures due for publication. But, when the Financial Services Bill finishes its parliamentary progress and the Board is duly designated as the regulatory agency, the changes themselves will not happen suddenly. There will be a specific day when the watchdog is given its teeth, but almost all areas of the investment industry are already anticipating that day by their own actions.

Although the details of the pending rules are vital, the broad aim of the entire system is both clear and logical. Companies have consequently been able to take the first steps towards fitting in with the expected new requirements, through measures such as the appointment of 'compliance officers' to ensure that all employees of an investment business know, understand and comply with, both the existing rules and new ones to be introduced.

A wide variety of investment businesses have been examining the way that possible conflicts of interest can arise from dealing and other procedures and have taken their own steps to build the curious edifices, now popularly known as Chinese Walls, against them. In many cases companies have themselves already been able to identify the kind of danger areas that the board will have to provide against, and are taking early action to deal with them. If it were not for the difficulties that some businesses have encountered in getting underwriting support, there would by now have been considerably more progress in setting up compensation schemes as well, an area where we hope to be able to provide considerable assistance shortly.

Before the details of the new requirements are available, the markets do have some existing examples to use as general guidance. The Stock Exchange has had its own long-standing compensation scheme and an effective compliance department, complete with roving inspectors for several years. The London Metal Exchange has decided to go for a clearing house of its own before any requirement forces it to do so. With so much work ahead for the entire financial community, facing the near-simultaneous events of the Financial Services Bill, pensions and building societies legislation and the effects of the Big Bang on The Stock Exchange community, intelligent anticipation can help the industry over the worst of the traumas now upon us all. Certainly any inclination to sit back and wait until the last moment will be a dangerous policy. A moment will not be enough and, under the Bill, neither we nor any self-regulatory organisation we may recognise, will have the right to authorise investment business which does not meet the standards required.

The relationship of the SIB to the SROs is fairly clear-cut. We expect there to be only four or five SROs, each of which will be concerned solely with investment business over a particular range of activities. Our relationship with recognised professional bodies is less straightforward. In the first place, there are many more of them – at least a dozen groups of accountants, solicitors, actuaries, chartered surveyors, etc., are potentially in a position to put themselves forward for recognition under the Act.

Secondly, investment business is not the main concern of their members and their rule books, governing bodies and disciplinary arrangements are not set up with investment business primarily in mind. The changes required of them under the Financial Services Bill may not be welcome – or indeed easy to apply.

But the new system of investor protection is expected, to use the usual cliché, to ensure a level playing field in which investment business, wherever carried out, is subject to equivalent rules and adequate monitoring and disciplinary arrangements. I quite understand the difficulties which professional bodies may have in adjusting their systems to meet the business activities of a minority of their members and the unwelcome prospect that the SIB may, in the last analysis, have to insist on a rule change in the investment area of a very old established and chartered RPB in the same way as it may have to do for an SRO. But if the bill requires equal protection for investors in all markets, we need powers to be able to ensure that this principle be applied. Those who take the benefits of recognition must take the responsibilities too. It may be that these powers would be able to recognise the special position of professional bodies. But additional powers there must be. It is, after all, always open to a professional body not to ask for recognition and to leave its members to seek authorisation for their investment business from an SRO or from the SIB itself. Indications are that some of the dozen or so professional bodies who are entitled to seek recognition are likely to take this alternative course.

We have had some surprises ourself in the passage of the Bill so far. The very last day of the committee stage left us a criminal prosecution authority, a particularly unusual function for a private limited company. But we can see that there is considerable logic to the idea that, since we will be operating a system which makes the carrying on of unauthorised investment business a criminal offence, we should be able to prosecute those who break that law or who attempt to gain authorisation fraudulently. No good watchdog has reason to complain about getting a strong set of teeth.

But it was a reminder, if we needed one, that the Bill itself can still change our areas of responsibility and the powers to deal with them. The report stage of the Bill in the House of Commons will take place very shortly and several issues, including the clarification of our own status as the designated agency and the vexed issue of the appeal by self-regulatory bodies for some form of immunity from claims for damages – a case in which we have considerable sympathy – look likely to be debated.

It may be that we have to accept the fact that any efficient regulator, or prospective regulator, is unlikely to be universally beloved by those to be regulated. But we are very ready to listen, both now when the rules are being drawn up in draft form and later when they are in practice. I hope John Bullock of Deloitte's would agree that we were able to come to a reasonable compromise with his own profession about an auditor's rights and duties in reporting possible problems. This is a consultative process and if we can be assured that alternatives to our own original suggestions can achieve the desired result and will be more practicable then we have no intention of ignoring them. But we must be quite satisfied that that result can be reached. Settling for second-best for the sake of a quiet life would be failing in our duty as a designated agency. I doubt very much whether we would be doing anybody, practitioner or customer, much of a favour by doing that.

4   Preparing for the Big Bang

Philip Wilkinson
Group Chief Executive, National Westminster Bank PLC

Moving again from the regulator's to the practitioner's viewpoint Philip
Wilkinson describes National Westminster Bank's response to the new
market environment. This he characterises as a policy of financial diversification via selective acquisitions, contrasting with Lloyd's preference for
building up its own in-house expertise and Barclay's more ambitious
acquisition programme. Mr Wilkinson expects there to be only ten
major players in London's financial markets by 1990 and National
Westminster's strategy is to ensure that it is among these survivors of the
Big Bang.

Big Bang can mean a lot of different things: a loud noise, a sudden
explosion, even the origins of the Universe. And I believe it is entirely
appropriate to use these two words to describe the changes taking place
in London's financial markets. These changes have certainly generated a
great deal of sound and fury and they will create a new world for financial
services.

The fuse for the Big Bang has been burning slowly since 1983 when
The Stock Exchange agreed to abolish fixed commissions in return for
the Office of Fair Trading dropping its action in the Restrictive Practices
Court against certain Stock Exchange rules. Though few, if any, realised
it at the time, this deal meant the end of single capacity and led to opening
up membership of The Stock Exchange to outside institutions. So, the
agreement paved the way for banks to play their part in the revolution
taking place in financial markets. But there were already underlying
forces at work which made commercial banks and Stock Exchange firms
look seriously at what each could offer the other.

The underlying forces?

If the 1970s was the decade of the international credit markets, then the 1980s is set to be the decade of the international capital markets. Banks were centre-stage in the 1970s as they channelled OPEC surpluses to corporations, institutions and countries hungry for funds.

In the 1980s, international capital surpluses come not just from the Middle East but from the Far East, that is Japan. Lending to countries outside the first division has lost its attractions in the wake of the sovereign debt problem, and the Japanese look to the stock markets of London, Europe and the United States as channels for investment. The dominant international investors now favour the capital markets. The top corporate, institutional and sovereign borrowers also prefer to do business there. Bonds and Note Issuance Facilities have replaced the Syndicated Eurocurrency Credit as their preferred source of finance.

Having been centre-stage in the 1970s, the banks were faced with the unwelcome prospect of being relegated to the wings in the 1980s. Therefore, it was natural for banks to respond positively to the resurgence of the capital markets and to make plans to meet this new challenge in world finance.

If banks were watching developments in the financial world closely, then so too were the world's securities markets, none more so than in the City of London. Under the impact of technology, the liberalisation of financial markets and the growing sophistication of customers, we are moving rapidly to the creation of one global securities market, operating around the clock. The global market will be based on the three legs of New York, Tokyo and London, linked through their respective time zones by the latest technology. London's position in the world arena is becoming more important and yet more threatened. The very attractiveness of London, particularly since the abolition of Exchange Control in 1979, has led to an invasion by American Securities Houses and banks. They have been joined more recently by Japanese and European institutions.

This invasion was bound to lead to new groupings. I do not believe that many Stock Exchange firms could have hoped to survive in the new world on their own. Banks may have been ardent suitors but many Stock Exchange firms also realised the dangers of being left on the shelf. The brokers and jobbers gladly embraced their new partners, who can supply them with the capital, the client relationships and the international network they need to compete effectively against the big battalions of the US and Japan. So the arrangements between Stock Exchange firms and outside institutions have been true marriages, each party furnishing skills and strengths which complement the other.

Fundamental changes in the financial world, and the agreement between The Stock Exchange and the Government, gave NatWest the motivation and the opportunity to play a significant role in London's capital markets. It is determined to maintain its position as an international financial services group and could not afford to let the opportunity pass by. Particularly when it could put to use the strength of its capital base, its client list and its international network. It has relationships with most of the world's major corporations and is represented in 35 countries, including naturally all the major financial centres of the world. What's more it was not sailing into totally unchartered waters when contemplating entering the capital markets.

Much is made of the clash of cultures between commercial and investment banks, yet the underlying philosophy of the capital markets – that of risk-taking and market-making – is not alien to NatWest. Through forex and money market operations, NatWest is experienced in taking positions. It should not be forgotten that it was closely involved in the early stages of LIFFE (London International Financial Futures Exchange). The subsidiary, NatWest Financial Futures Ltd, now has five seats on the trading floor and is a major player in what is an increasingly important market.

NatWest has a trading as well as a lending culture. Even before the Big Bang was first contemplated, it already had capital market expertise building up within the Group. County Bank, the Group's merchant bank – a successful merchant bank in its own right since the late 1960s – is a major player in the Eurobond market, where it originates, distributes and trades securities. In effect, County acts as a banker, a broker and a jobber. County is also heavily involved with The London Stock Exchange as both supplier and customer as an issuing house and an investment manager. It was natural to use County Bank as a firm foundation for the capital markets operations which are being brought together in NatWest Investment Bank (NWIB). Start-up capital of £300 million makes NWIB one of the top capital markets groups announced so far, and is a sign of our determination to become a significant force in investment banking.

The German and Swiss subsidiaries, Deutsche Westminster Bank and HandelsBank are active in their domestic capital markets and will also contribute to NatWest's international securities ambitions.

As a leading international financial services group, NatWest aims to have a 24-hour dealing capability across the three main financial time zones, to become one of the top five investment banks in the UK and to be a major player in the leading capital markets of the world in the USA, Europe and the Far East.

We have built up our capital market capability through a combination of existing strengths, acquisitions and *de novo* operations. In London, we have acquired full control of Fielding Newson-Smith, stockbrokers and County Bisgood, stockjobbers. We have built a new team to deal in international equities, County Securities, and a new market maker in gilt edged securities, which begins trading in October. Securities trading teams in London will link with counterparts in Hong Kong and Australia. In both centres, we have established a merchant banking capability. We have also acquired Watson & Co., a stockbroking firm in Hong Kong. We are applying for a securities licence in Tokyo and intend to establish a securities operation in New York as soon as local regulations are more favourable.

The Clearing Banks have adopted different strategies as we move towards the Big Bang. Our approach to building a capital markets organisation lies somewhere between that employed by Lloyds and Barclays: the former is building up its own expertise whilst Barclays' acquisitions have been on a more ambitious scale than our own. Having seen County bank grow organically throughout the 1970s, we were sympathetic to the concept of creating a home grown capital markets organisation. But we felt it would be hard to bed down teams recruited from a variety of sources and to rear in-house expertise in the short time available prior to Big Bang.

We noted also the experience of New York following the US equivalent of the Big Bang – 'Mayday 1975'. If London follows the same path, there will probably be, in five years time, ten major players with 60–70 per cent of the business. Those ten major players will include many of our banking competitors. If we are not a serious competitor in the business by 1990, it may be very difficult to break in afterwards. Therefore, we considered that selective acquisitions were the best way forward. Yet, although we are not unambitious, our acquisitions have, for a variety of reasons, been of medium-sized brokers and jobbers. We wanted to minimise the goodwill payment which is based on earnings achieved by brokers and jobbers in a protected environment. We also wanted to minimise the problems of integration. One of the problems that is often mentioned in this context is the high level of pay which some people are commanding in the present competitive situation. Skilled and experienced people are the basis of any successful business and the very best are in great demand. Certainly our Group employs some expensive people; but only where we are convinced that their contribution will justify their remuneration.

One thing is quite clear: integration is easier in an environment of growth rather than rationalisation. In fact, one or two investment banks have already found that their ambitions have out-run their purse and talk of cutbacks is emerging. We felt that what is needed for success is a spirit of enthusiasm and that can only be created in an expanding situation. The relative size of Fieldings and Bisgoods on the one hand and County Bank on the other, mean that it will be relatively easy to create a new Group identity in NWIB. To borrow an idea from the world of physics . . . which is not out of place as we look forward to Big Bang, our target is a 'minimum critical mass', making for a viable operation in each market.

We believe that the middle way gains most advantages while avoiding the worst of the pitfalls.

I have described our motives for entering the capital markets, our strategic aims and how we set about building our capital markets operation. How will all this strengthen our business?

I see three specific ways in which the growing expertise and skills of NatWest Investment bank will benefit the whole Group: firstly, in our corporate services; secondly, in our retail services; and thirdly, in creating new products.

The greatest benefit is to provide, as a Group, a more complete range of corporate services. The NWIB marketing effort will complement the strength of our international and domestic network of relationships with the top corporates of the world. The aim is to add the growing range of capital-based services to our existing credit-based products and to use the Group's existing marketing channels to make the most of their relationship strengths. The proposals for a UK Sterling Commercial paper market open new doors for us.

Secondly, I see a big opportunity to involve NWIB in our retail personal services through our United Kingdom branch network. The Government's campaign for wider share ownership which was given further encouragement in the recent Budget and the deluge of press information about the whole field of Stock Exchange investments has struck a chord with the general public. We aim to grasp the opportunity as individuals become more confident investors. Our aim is to sell stocks, shares and other investments through the branches. The Personal Equity Plans proposed in the Budget open new avenues in investment management for the banks.

The third opporunity for the Group lies in creating new, convenient product packages. One example would be an Asset Management Service for our more wealthy customers. That service would bring together overdraft facilities, investment management services, unit trusts, insurance services, tax and a credit card in a variety of combinations to enhance our product range. This package has been possible before, of course, with the assistance of outside brokers and dealers. But the point is we can cut the cloth to suit ourselves now, and share neither customers nor profit with other institutions. I see no reason why banks cannot act with the same discretion as that claimed by other investment portfolio managers and I need hardly stress that Sir Kenneth Berrill should have no worries about NatWest operating within both the spirit and the letter of the law. We shall be vigilant in avoiding conflicts of interest.

The changes that we are seeing in the world's financial markets are in response to fundamental and, I believe, irreversible forces. I am confident that London will emerge as a stronger financial centre as a result of the changes. Investors too will benefit through cheaper and more efficient dealing in a wider range of investment instruments. For those institutions jockeying for position in the capital markets, undoubtedly there are risks and uncertainties in what is sure to be an extremely competitive marketplace. Predictions that there will be 'blood on the streets' are commonplace, and the Big Bang will inevitably produce casualties. The Bank of America has decided that the risks of becoming involved in the emerging market are too high. Others may reach the same conclusion, but any bank wishing to remain a leader in the first division cannot just stand aside.

5 A supervisor's perspective on deregulation

Rodney Galpin
Executive Director, Bank of England

While Sir Kenneth Berrill's regulatory responsibilities cover the securities industry Rodney Galpin carries responsibility for supervising the UK banking system. However, with banking and securities activities being merged in conglomerate organisations the new financial marketplace will require careful co-ordination between supervisory authorities. Mr Galpin here addresses the dangers of regulatory overlap and underlap in a situation where banks are operating not only across different sectors of the financial services industry but also across national boundaries.

I am conscious as a banking supervisor that an understanding of the competitive pressures which banks are likely to face, as well as the commercial opportunities which Big Bang will provide, are important to the process and the development of banking supervision. Undoubtedly there will be risks. It is perhaps axiomatic to say that business opportunities always carry risk but the opportunities now opening up to banks seem to me to carry risks not all of which are yet quantifiable. Supervision will, therefore, have to be rigorous but tempered with sensitivity and an understanding of the practical world in such a way as to preserve for the practitioners themselves the benefits which the opportunities should bring. An orderly system of supervision should be of benefit to us all.

The changes which are occurring are wider than those related to the opening up of the UK securities markets. I intend in this section to describe these wider changes which together are influencing the attitudes and structures of banking institutions. It would be too wide a canvas to cover all the implications of these changes and I shall be seeking to concentrate on the risks involved, from the standpoint of a banking supervisor, in the area of securities business undertaken by banks.

The changes which the banks now face stem from a number of factors:

1   Deregulation notably in the United States of America [see sections 1 and 8].
2   The introduction of new technology, enabling information to flow accurately and instantaneously around the world.
3   Much greater sophistication among corporate treasurers, many of whom work in multinational companies.
4   A highly competitive environment.

At a time when banks' capital ratios have been under pressure, their need is to satisfy the requirements of their clients, and maintain their own profitability, without unduly inflating their balance sheets; in consequence, banks are increasingly beginning to introduce – in competition with non-banks – product packages and a range of services, often tailor-made and offered at least cost and with the maximum of flexibility; in many cases the risks surrounding these activities are carried off-balance sheet.

Talk of disintermediation, securitisation and innovation in banking services has become a staple diet at many luncheon tables. The gradual removal of barriers in many countries to the flow of capital across national boundaries adds to the competitive pressures. Those competitive challenges are made no easier by the move towards greater disclosure in a bank's account of the detail of its activities. Comparison of performance with that of other banks thus becomes easier. As we have seen, banks are not immune from takeover and they are consequently under greater pressure from shareholders than in the past. These influences are not, of course, unique to the United Kingdom.

What is perhaps unique here is the combination of these changes with the decision to remove the barriers to entry which had previously prevented large new participants from entering into the UK securities markets. This has led to a number of institutional marriages arranged to equip the partners collectively to react to, and benefit from, the opportunities created by this relaxation and the other changes I have referred to. Many of these have involved banks, since, in the United Kingdom, there is no statutory impediment, such as a Glass-Steagall Act, to a bank engaging in securities business. New risks are being created and it is with these that banking supervisors, as well as individual banks, have to come to terms.

Let me now turn to the risks to banks which I see as arising directly from the restructuring of the securities markets. First of all some institutions may be entering into business which is new to them. They are having to recruit new people in an environment where demand exceeds supply. They are having, in many cases, to assimilate and bring together a variety of different cultures. This is by no means easy and involves creating the right balance between effective reporting lines and controls and the need to preserve the motivation of those whose experience in certain markets has been the reason for their assimilation. Perhaps the evidence which has been seen of individuals, or groups of individuals, moving to other institutions soon after their business has been acquired is evidence of this difficulty. Markets are being reorganised – the gilt-edged market for instance – and following Big Bang it seems certain that the players in the markets will encounter aggressive competition. They are having to install new systems and introduce expensive new technology with some speed. They are going to have to compete not just domestically, but more importantly, internationally. All these carry risks, even if they are of an unquantifiable nature. It will not be until markets have had time to settle down that we shall know with hindsight how large these risks really are.

Banking Supervision has as its objectives the protection of depositors' interests and the effectiveness of the banking system itself. The latter is important because banking is an industry in which confidence is a crucial ingredient. It is this confidence factor – a principal characteristic of banks but not so important for other types of institution – which creates special problems for a bank supervisor. Let me give point to this statement. Banks are vulnerable to liquidity pressures and experience has shown that there can be considerable difficulty in isolating problems in one part of a bank's business from its deposit-taking activities, particularly where the bank concerned may rely heavily on the wholesale markets. Any extension of activity into new areas and products must carry additional risk which banks, more than most, have to weigh carefully. Securities operations are no exception.

Some banks already conduct a securities activity from their own balance sheets. The contagion risks involved are consequently not wholly unknown to bank supervisors in the Unitied Kingdom. We do not, however, necessarily have any less concern about them where the securities activity is carried out, not on a bank's own balance sheet, but through a separately capitalised and specialised securities company within a group of which a bank is part. This may be particularly true where the group as a whole conducts its business in companies carrying the name of the bank. A number of such financial groupings have already been formed.

It seems certain that a large part of the funding of securities activity will come from the banking sector. Where this funding is to an unrelated company no new problems arise from a banking supervisory angle. Depositors' interests are protected by the supervisor's approach to, and treatment of, the incidence and concentration of risk in a bank's assets. It is likely, however, that in a financial conglomerate the bank in the group will wish, for wholly understandable commercial reasons, to fund its related securities company. This will pose a supervisory problem in relation to large exposures. The Bank sees 10 per cent of a bank's capital base as the threshold for the specific reporting of large exposures and, as already stated publicly, 25 per cent of capital is to become the maximum exposure to which, except in exceptional circumstances, banks will be expected to lend to any one client, or group of connected clients.

Experience very clearly shows that an over-concentration of lending in one area is more often than not a significant factor which detracts from a bank's capacity to withstand losses. Is it appropriate, the banking supervisor has to ask himself, for a bank's funding of a related company, or group of related companies, to be less rigorously treated than any other large exposure? The problem is compounded by the connected nature of the lending in such cases, and it is here that the question of contagion between various parts of a financial group, to which I referred earlier, becomes a relevant consideration.

I have referred to some of the implications for our treatment of large exposures which may arise from inter-group funding between a bank and its related securities business. In devising our large exposure rules we are well aware of the need to consider also the question of underwriting – a business already undertaken by our merchant banks, but one which with the growth of bought deals is likely to add to the credit risks associated with such activities. We have also to consider the position of those banks which act, as it were, as wholesalers in Eurobond and other issues, trading as market makers in those instruments. In both these areas we are also considering how to balance the containment of credit risk with the need to preserve equal competition between institutions operating in these areas.

I have no answer now to these issues but we are thinking hard about them and hope to issue shortly a consultative paper on large exposures which will address the whole range of issues related to the concentration of risk. That paper will deal with all the affiliate issues involved and describe the concessions to its general policy which the Bank feels should be allowed.

The remarks I have just made are relevant, of course, to our concern about the interests of depositors. But there are also issues which touch upon the effectiveness of the banking system – the second of the objectives which a banking supervisor seeks to meet. The need to ensure that potential conflicts of interest between investment and dealing operations, or with other activities undertaken by banks, are recognised and avoided through proper internal disciplines and controls is one important supervisory concern. It is not, of course, confined to banking supervision. Market reputation – and thus confidence – can be affected by confusion in the minds of clients about the precise identity of the institution with which they are dealing. There is also a danger that the credibility of market-making services may be undermined if it is seen that dealing in these areas is not independent from other dealing activities. The Bank has traditionally been concerned from a supervisory aspect in the organisation of a bank's dealing operations – and it will continue to have such a concern. This is not to say that dealing in a number of activities cannot be carried out in one dealing room. Where this happens the Bank will, however, want to ensure that the back office functions can cope with that dealing structure. It is important that dual treasury functions for banking and securities businesses within a group should be so structured and controlled as to avoid counterparty confusion which might lead to limits for individual group companies being inadvertently broadened. The market itself has an important role to play here in developing conventions which minimise the risk of counterparty confusion.

I should like to turn now to the possibility of overlap and underlap in the supervision of financial activities and in particular of bank conglomerates. Both need to be avoided as far as possible: overlap because it might create confusion and add to compliance costs and underlap because it would mean that in relation to certain activities the interests of those to whom the relevant supervisors had their prime duty were being inadequately assessed. A bank which engages in securities business on its own balance sheet will need dual authorisation – from the Bank of England under the Banking Act and from an SRO (or the SIB itself). This dual authorisation could result in an overlap in supervision, as indeed could also the concerns of a number of different regulatory bodies in the supervision of the activities of a financial conglomerate, since different regulators will have their own, perhaps differing, requirements particularly as regards capital for the activities they supervise. I have said that overlap needs to be avoided as far as possible and it is in part for this reason that it is proposed that supervisors should be given statutory authority to exchange relevant information. It is also intended to introduce arrangements, of an extra-statutory nature, for the co-ordination of the regulation of financial conglomerates. Co-operation between supervisors is also necessary to avoid regulatory underlap. It will normally be essential in a group structure to measure capital adequacy on a consolidated basis. Inadequacy of group capital can put the interests of depositors or investors at risk and it seems to me important, therefore, that account should be taken on a consolidated basis of the activities of all the companies, either here or abroad, which are part of a supervised institution.

The concept has been proposed of a lead regulator whose responsibility it will be to bring together the various regulators responsible within the UK for the activities of parts of the group, and to ensure each supervisor is as fully informed as possible about the overall financial condition of the group and its corporate aims. No system of co-operation can remove from any regulatory body its own particular statutory responsibility. No supervisory system can guarantee that there will not be failures and anyone who makes such an assertion is, I fear, living in a fool's paradise; but supervision should clearly help to minimise the risk of failure. To that extent it will be of comfort in relation to the risk of contagion to know that those parts of a financial group which are supervised within the United Kingdom will benefit from the lead regulator concept which I have described. But risks will still remain, more particularly where the group concerned has operations around the world, perhaps in countries where the supervisory regime is less well developed.

Co-operation will also be necessary between supervisors for the purpose of seeking some consistency of approach in the standards applied and creating playing fields which are reasonably level and do not distort competition. The increasing internationalism of market players, many of whom will have operations elsewhere as well as in the United Kingdom, make this a somewhat daunting task and will necessitate the development of co-operation on an international basis, a process which started as far as banking supervision is concerned in the mid-1970s through meetings in Basle of supervisors from the Group of ten countries. The international co-ordination of supervision will be no easy task. It will have to take into account not only the variety of functions being supervised, for example, banking, securities dealing and insurance, but also the different legal and accounting regimes which different countries apply. It will be no easier to evaluate how level playing fields are in an international context.

So far I have stressed some of the problems, or rather challenges, which deregulation will produce and have produced few concrete answers to them. It is right that I should now say what I, as a banking supervisor, regard as the principal areas to be addressed by both banks and their supervisors. I do so in fairly general terms.

A large part of responsibility rests with the chairman and senior management in the institutions involved. It seems to me that they should do three things:

1   They should make sure they understand the risks their institution runs and that the institution continues to have regard to credit risk which it has hitherto been left largely to banks to assess. Innovative developments now taking place may leave no one making such

assessments; credit committees in banks should I suggest concern themselves about this.

2   They should install systems and controls which measure those risks and enable them to be controlled; it is important that senior management assess for themselves the effectiveness of their control systems, using as appropriate for this purpose internal inspection, reporting to an Audit Committee independent of line management.

3   They should appoint compliance officers with reporting lines, as is already usual for internal inspection, directly to them or to the bank's audit committee; and they should be prepared to act vigorously in stamping out any abuses which the compliance officer brings to their attention.

The Bank of England for its part would be failing in its duty if it did not attempt to point out the risks involved and set in place regulatory procedures to limit excessive risk-taking. The Bank's recent paper on off-balance sheet exposure, published soon after an international paper produced by the Cooke Committee in Basle, is an example of the consultative approach which we intend to take with many of these issues. Another will be the large exposure paper to which I have previously referred. But we shall not fail to act decisively and vigorously to limit excessive risk-taking which we consider may dangerously affect depositors' interests or the stability of the banking system. An example of such action may be seen in the notice issued to banks in February in relation to bank participations in bids and mergers. I recognise the argument that it may be to the British banks' competitive disadvantage if supervisory practice here moves towards tighter supervision before any other. The argument can be overstated, but it would be wrong to ignore it. The fact is that the United Kingdom is an important financial centre in which innovation and changing practices within banks are increasingly prevalent. There seems to me to be no sense in allowing practices which raise unacceptable risks for depositors or the system as a whole to continue here: it is against this consideration that the Bank must assess the need to introduce new supervisory techniques and I am sure we shall find that other banking supervisors will not be far behind.

In conclusion I would say that we are moving into exciting and challenging times in which banks will be out to seize new business opportunities through innovation and their involvement in new markets. As a supervisory authority the Bank does not want this to involve excessive risk-taking which would jeopardise depositors' interests or the effectiveness of the banking system. The Bank wants healthy, vital markets; it has no desire to obstruct innovation unnecessarily; it wants to encourage fair competition through playing fields which are as level as it is prudent to be. To achieve all this there is a need for co-operation between supervisors and between the market participants and their regulators.

Co-operation must involve consultation. The latter should not, however, be in only one direction. It is as important for banks to consult their supervisors before entering into new practices or adopting innovative techniques, as it is for the supervisor to consult the banks about the supervisory techniques he is proposing to introduce. The system of banking supervision in the United Kingdom is flexible by nature and, although statutorily based, it does not involve the incorporation into legislation of a host of supervisory ratios and practices which can only be changed by amending regulation – for which it may be difficult to find parliamentary time. An over legalised system would destroy much of the flexibility which is now characteristic of our system and beneficial, in my judgement, to the interests of both the supervisor and the institutions he supervises. We can still, I am glad to say, rely on institutions working as much to the spirit as to the letter of the law. I very much hope that this attitude will continue unabated.

My final remark is that supervision neither is, nor should attempt to be, a substitute for competent and prudent management. It is for management to recognise and control the risks they run. I hope that we shall be able to assist them in achieving this objective.

6 The audit role in the context of financial deregulation

John Bullock

at Deloitte, Haskins, and Sells

The UK regulatory authorities have been leaning on the auditing profession to assist them in the supervisory process, particularly in the area of fraud. John Bullock argues that auditors are not generally in a position to detect or prevent fraud; that a duty (as against a right) to report relevant information to supervisors could present serious problems; and that reporting to supervisors without prior knowledge of the client would breach the traditional confidentiality relationship.

The new regulatory framework for the financial services sector is beginning to fall into place. One of the most contentious areas still to be resolved concerns the role of the auditor. There are several specific issues which are causing particular concern at the moment. Before discussing recent developments in the auditor's role, it might be helpful if I first summarise the conceptual role of auditing in the corporate sector in general.

The conceptual role of auditing

An audit consists of an independent examination of, and report on, a company's financial statements. The report, which is addressed to the company's shareholders, expresses an opinion on whether the financial statements show a true and fair view and comply with the Companies Act. The need for auditing arises because there is often a separation between those who own a company (the shareholders) and those who manage the company (the directors).

Company law in the UK sets out a framework of accountability, in which the directors are required to prepare a report and accounts that give a true and fair view of the financial position and performance of the company. This reporting mechanism gives the shareholders an opportunity to assess the stewardship and success of the directors in managing the business entrusted to them. The shareholders can then hold the directors accountable for their performance. There are often reasons why directors could be subject to some bias in the way in which the results of their management are presented. If there were no independent attestation of the accounts that the directors present, then the shareholders might doubt the fairness of the accounts.

So the auditor's role is to provide comfort to the shareholders that the accounts do show a true and fair view of the company's results and state of affairs. The independent audit adds credibility to the financial information that the directors publish. The auditor therefore performs a monitoring function in maintaining proper accountability in the corporate sector. This view of accountability might be termed the traditional one, in which the directors are considered to be accountable to the shareholders only. This is the traditional view, in which the directors prepare the financial statements for the shareholders, and the auditor addresses his report to the shareholders. However, for many years the auditing profession has recognised that the audit report is relied on by other parties (that is, not just by the shareholders). For example, lenders (such as banks) and government departments (such as the Inland Revenue) have relied to some extent on unqualified audit reports as a means of indirectly verifying the figures in a company's accounts.

So there is a wider view of accountability, which holds that the directors owe a duty not just to a shareholder but to anyone who entrusts resources to the care of the directors. So in this wider view of accountability the directors would be accountable to shareholders, lenders, creditors, employees and even to the general public if the directors are considered to have control over some of the country's human and physical resources. In this wider view of accountability, the auditors would take into account the concerns of all these potential users of the financial statements. This would imply that the auditors should not necessarily address their report to the shareholders only. We have perhaps seen a move over the last few decades from the narrow traditional view of accountability towards this wider view, in which directors and auditors must take account of the concerns of third parties, other than the shareholders. However, few people in the profession would take the extreme view that auditors should take into account all the concerns of all potential users of the accounts. I would certainly not go that far.

Whatever view of accountability you take, it is clear that one of the key features of the auditing function is independence. The auditor's authority and credibility stem from his independence from management and from any particular group of shareholders. Financial independence is vital – the economic well-being of an auditing firm must not have undue dependence on the activities of any one particular client. The ethical guidelines of the professional bodies emphasise how important it is for the auditor to be independent – and to be seen to be independent. So the auditor can express his opinion on the client's accounts without fear or favour.

Another key feature of the auditing function is confidentiality. The auditor is normally aware of sensitive information about the company's activities and future plans. The company's management would be reluctant to communicate freely with the auditor if they believed that the auditor would divulge sensitive information to third parties. The profession's ethical guidelines include specific rules on confidentiality.

So the auditing function is an important element in the framework of corporate accountability. However, I want to make it clear that an auditor is not the same as a supervisor. The distinction is particularly important in the new regulatory system in the financial services sector. The auditor focuses on a financial period which has passed, whereas the supervisor focuses on the present. The auditor might only visit his client in the month or two either side of the year-end, whereas the supervisor has a day-to-day monitoring responsibility. And finally, the auditor is not required to assess or comment on the competence or behaviour of the directors and other management.

The profession wants to ensure that the new regulatory system distinguishes properly between the role of the supervisor and the role of the auditor. The supervisor would be either the Secretary of State, or the SIB or the relevant self-regulating organisation (SRO). The profession considers that management has the primary responsibility for the proper conduct of the business. The supervisor's role is to see that management discharges that responsibility. The supervisor will establish specific rules and regulations that management will have to comply with. The auditor then provides additional support for the supervisor in helping to ensure that these requirements are met. The DTI does not expect auditors 'to carry out a major part of the regulatory burden'. However, the proposed system would involve new obligations on auditors in order to meet the DTI's objective of facilitating communication between auditors and supervisors.

At this stage, I should make some reference to fraud. The auditor is not responsible for preventing fraud. And indeed, he is not in a position to prevent fraud. Nor is he responsible for detecting fraud (unless the fraud results in the accounts not showing a true and fair view, or not complying with the Companies Act). The general public may consider that the auditor is a financial policeman, who is responsible for preventing crime and for detecting it. However, the Government and the accounting profession are generally in agreement that the auditor is not responsible for preventing or for detecting fraud.

The profession believes that the most effective way of preventing fraud is through proper systems of internal control and management information. The new regulatory system for the financial services sector will require investment businesses to establish proper control systems. Auditors can provide a service to clients by advising them on how to satisfy the requirements, by checking that suitable controls are in place and by reporting weaknesses and breakdowns to management. However, it is management who has the prime responsibility for preventing fraud and for ensuring that satisfactory internal controls are in place. I shall talk later about the auditor's responsibilities for reporting fraud. The reporting issue is a contentious one at the moment.

This brief summary of the conceptual role of auditing has introduced two important issues which I shall discuss in detail later. However, it might be useful to identify the issues at this stage. Both issues concern the problem the auditor has in identifying the priorities among the parties to whom he is responsible. Firstly, in the context of illegal acts – and also in other contexts – there is the specific difficulty of identifying what action should be taken when the interests of customers or depositors may differ from those of shareholders. Secondly, there is the problem of how the auditor should use confidential information, if his responsibility to his immediate client conflicts with his broad professional obligation to society at large. I shall return to these issues later.

Current developments in the financial services sector

I have so far addressed the conceptual role of auditing. The legal, social and political factors that influence the auditing role will change over time. For example, in recent years we have seen a new requirement for the auditor to review the Directors Report, as well as the accounts themselves. And in the audit of local authorities, we have seen an increased emphasis on aspects of fraud, and on reviewing whether rate-payers get value for money. So the perception of the auditor's responsibilities is dynamic, not static.

The financial services sector in particular has seen significant recent developments in the concepts of the auditor's role.

Developments are occurring on three fronts, namely:
1   banks
2   building societies
3   financial services in general.
The government's concern in these areas has been prompted by failures

of the existing regulatory system – as in Johnson Matthey Bank and
Grays Building Society, for example.

In the banking sector, the Government has recently issued a White
Paper on 'Banking Supervision'. The White Paper proposes that auditors
should, in exceptional cases, contact the supervisory authorities without
the knowledge of the client. 'Exceptional cases' would include suspected
management fraud, for example. In building societies, the Government
has recently published the Building Societies Bill. The Bill's proposals
would remove the auditor's normal confidentiality requirement in
certain circumstances. These circumstances are not specified in the Bill,
but might include suspected management fraud.

In addition to these proposals in specific sectors, the Government has
published the Financial Services Bill, which is aimed at establishing a
whole new framework for protecting the investor and for regulating
investment businesses. Although the Bill itself does not include any
provisions relating to auditors, there is considerable debate at present as
to precisely how the auditing profession should contribute to the new
regulatory framework for investment businesses. The debate has involved discussion between the DTI, the Securities and Investments Board
(SIB) and the professional accountancy bodies. The recent discussion has
been largely based on the DTI Consultative Document on 'The auditor's
role in the financial services sector', which the DTI issued in January 1986.

The Financial Services Bill does not include any provisions relating to
auditors. However, the consultative process will no doubt give rise to
specific provisions, which will then be put forward as Government
amendments in the course of the Bill's passage through Parliament. The
Bill has gone through the committee stage, and is now moving on to the
report stage, before going to the House of Lords. (The Bill has so far
remained relatively unscathed in its passage through the Commons, but
it is as well to remember the rough passage of the Insolvency Bill in the
House of Lords last year.) The Government hopes that the new legislation will be in place by the end of the year.

The DTI Consultative Document outlines the basis of the proposed
relationship between auditors and supervisors. The Consultative
Document says that the auditor would have to notify the supervisors of
specific events, such as a decision to resign or to qualify the accounts.
And the auditor would have a more general duty 'to co-operate with the
supervisors'. It seems to me (and, I believe, to the profession at large) that
this general duty to 'co-operate' is extremely vague. Who defines what is
meant by 'co-operation'? Will the auditor's interpretation of the term be
the same as the DTI's? And how will the client define the term? In my
opinion, the proposal as it stands is likely to create confusion among
auditors and among their clients.

This leads to one of the key issues in the current debate. That is, should auditors have a duty to report relevant information to the supervisors, or should they have a right? The accounting profession is concerned that a duty to report would leave the auditors open to be sued if, with the benefit of hindsight, they could be accused of failing to report any relevant information to the supervisors. If an investment business collapsed, there would always be a danger that there was something that should have reported to the supervisors.

There would be several adverse consequences of a duty being imposed on auditors. Firstly, client management may be less willing than in the past to discuss sensitive issues with the auditor, for fear that the auditor will immediately disclose the information to the supervisors. The information flow from the client to the auditor may therefore dry up to some extent, thus making it more difficult for the auditor to perform his duty effectively. I want to emphasise that the auditor's task can only be performed if there is an unencumbered flow of information from the management of the client – so that the auditor may have all the evidence he requires to form his opinion. Anything which would interfere with that flow of information is to be avoided. The information flow to the auditor is most likely to dry up in sensitive circumstances, such as if there is a breakdown in internal controls, or if there is a serious financial deterioration in the state of the business. So there is a danger that clients will fail to seek professional advice just when they need it most.

The second adverse consequence of a duty is that auditors might flood the supervisors with information, just to cover themselves against potential litigation. This flood of information could easily clog up the system, leaving the supervisors to shift through a mass of data in an attempt to identify significant information.

And a third consequence of a duty being imposed is that the fear of litigation may drive auditors away from the more risky end of the market – that is, away from the high-risk investment businesses that need an audit most. (The levels of litigation may increase if investment businesses consider that their business has suffered as a result of the auditor reporting confidential matters to the authorities without any justification. However, the auditors may well have a sufficient defence if he can say that he was merely fulfilling his legal duty to report.)

So the profession has argued strongly, on practical grounds, against a duty being imposed on the auditors to report relevant information to the supervisors. The profession believes that it would be more appropriate for auditors to have a right, not a duty, to report to the supervisors. The existence of a right would keep open the communication link to the supervisors, while giving the auditor room to exercise his professional judgement as to whether or not the information should be reported to the supervisors. The existence of a right would substantially reduce the auditor's fear of potential litigation. However, the auditor would of course (and quite properly) still be open to lawsuits arising from negligence, if his work falls below the professional standards expected of an auditor. Not only must auditors be familiar with their own professional auditing and accounting standards, but they must also be familiar with the relevant rules and regulations of other bodies where appropriate (such as The Stock Exchange, NASDIM, etc.).

If auditors have a right to report rather than a duty, then the profession can contribute to the smooth running of the new regulatory system by acting as a filter. That is, the auditor can apply his professional judgement to his knowledge of the client's activities, in order to determine whether or not the supervisors should be made aware of specific information. So instead of the supervisors being overloaded with irrelevant data (as might happen if a duty were imposed), the supervisors may wish to rely on the auditor to filter out the unnecessary information and provide only relevant information.

After a lengthy debate between the professional bodies, the SIB and the Department of Trade and Industry, it seems that agreement has been reached that auditors should have a right to report, not a duty. The SIB has agreed with the profession that a right to report will be sufficient, provided that the professional bodies produce satisfactory guidance on how auditors should exercise that right in practice. Officials at the DTI are understood to be sympathetic towards this view. The DTI Consultative Document suggests that authorised investment businesses should include in their contract with their auditors a provision waiving any confidentiality restrictions as regards communications with supervisors.

Other problems arise over contacts between auditors and supervisors. The Consultative Document suggests that 'contact between auditor and supervisors would normally be at the supervisor's initiative or at the instigation of the authorised business'. In normal circumstances, the auditor would raise his concerns with the client and then, if relevant, the auditor would suggest that the authorised business should contact the supervisors. The auditor should contact the supervisors if the business refuses to do so, or if it significantly delays doing so. In general, the Document suggests that the auditor should consider contacting the supervisor if he believes that the absence of contact could harm the interests of investors (as distinct from shareholders).

So in normal circumstance, the auditor will not initiate contact with the supervisor, but will communicate via the authorised business. However, the Consultative Document proposes that in exceptional circumstances, the auditor may consider it necessary to communicate directly with the relevant supervisor, without informing the client. I understand that the view is that the auditor should go to the supervisor in one or more of five instances, which should be set out in law.

These five instances are:

1   Failure of internal controls (where detrimental to the investor and where management has not taken steps to remedy the failure).
2   Significant deterioration in financial position.
3   Misleading information given to the supervisor, or failure to report important information.
4   Accounts to be qualified.
5   Suspected fraud by management.

Only in the last of these five instances (suspected fraud) should the auditor report to the supervisors without the client's knowledge. The SIB view is that reporting without the client's knowledge would be most rare and would form a small proportion of the already rare occasions when the auditor would be contacting the supervisors. Nevertheless, I must point out that the profession is concerned that the DTI proposals will damage auditor/client confidentiality.

For example, the Institute of Chartered Accountants of Scotland issued a paper in July 1985 on 'The auditor's role with regard to fraud and irregularities in the financial services industry'. This paper recommends that 'In certain circumstances an auditor should seek a meeting with representatives of the appropriate self-regulating body'. The paper recommends that such a meeting should take place 'with the full knowledge of the client'. In his recent report on fraud for the English Institute, Lord Benson states that the traditional confidentiality relationship must be maintained. Lord Benson considers that an auditor must only disclose information concerning the affairs of the company under audit if there is a legal or professional duty to do so and if he first informs the client of his intention to disclose.

The profession is also concerned that management may bring actions for damages against the auditors, where the auditors have reported suspected management fraud to the supervisors. The profession considers that the new legislation should embody the principle that reports of suspected fraud, made in good faith to the supervisors, would attract protection from actions for damages.

So we have still to resolve the issue of whether, and in what circumstances, the auditor should contact the supervisor without first informing the client. It is likely in this context that the SIB's conduct of business rules will require the proposed contractual arrangement to allow the auditor to contact the supervisor directly without the knowledge of the client, if the auditor considers this necessary or desirable to protect the interests of investors. So the auditor will have legal support for breaking the normal confidentiality rules.

In the proposed new system the auditors will need to have an effective forum for communicating with the directors of the business. Effective communication will be particularly necessary when the auditor wants to inform the client that he intends to contact the supervisors. It seems to me than an audit committee is a good way of establishing an effective line of communication between the auditors and the directors. An audit committee can provide an independent internal check on the activities of senior management. It allows the auditor to communicate with directors other than the finance director. And an audit committee can be particularly effective when it includes non-executive directors – that is, directors who are financially independent of the company and who are independent from the directors who are responsible for the day-to-day management of the company. The Scottish Institute's 1985 paper on fraud reached a similar conclusion. However, I appreciate that there may be difficulties in obtaining sufficient non-executive directors of the appropriate quality. Also, smaller companies, and unsuccessful companies, may not have the resources to establish an audit committee – although these are perhaps the companies that are in most need of an audit committee.

Another important point arises in the Consultative Document's reference to circumstances where shareholders might benefit at the expense of the interests of investors. 'Investors' in this context refers to those who use the business for investment advice or investment management or transactions. Because the whole regulatory system is designed to protect investors, it seems that the DTI expects the auditors to report the relevant details of such circumstances to the supervisors. This would be the case even though the auditor would have a contractual relationship with the shareholders of the investment business, not with the investors who use the business. The auditor would be expected to consider the need to keep supervisors informed of matters they need to be aware of to perform their functions.

This seems to be a lot to expect of the auditor. For example, it could mean the auditor would have to look out for, and then report, all occasions in which the company or its shareholders were receiving an unfair benefit at the expense of third party investors. For example, if a company charges commission rates well in excess of market rates then shareholders would be pleased to see the resultant higher profits. However, the interests of investors would be harmed, and so it seems that the auditor would have a duty to report to the supervisors. Does the government really mean to extend the auditor's responsibilities in such an open-ended way? I do not think so. However, there are specific circumstances – for example, the wrongful use of client money – where I believe it would be reasonable for the auditors to report to the supervisor.

So the auditor's reporting relationship to the supervisor may depend on his assessment of third party interests – that is, the interests of those other than his client. This is a significant extension to the auditor's traditional role. The extension may reflect the 'wider view' of accountability that I mentioned earlier, in that the auditors will now have to monitor the accountability of the directors to depositors and investors, not just to the shareholders of the investment business.

The auditor already has to accept that his responsibility extends beyond his immediate client. For example, his audit report may be read and relied on by potential shareholders as well as by existing shareholders. The new proposal, however, will incorporate important new responsibilities into the new regulatory framework for investment businesses. In future, the auditor will have to recognise that he has a special responsibility to depositors and investors, distinct from his traditional and primary responsibility to shareholders.

I believe that auditors cannot shirk these new responsibilities. The auditing profession recognises that it owes a professional duty to society at large, as well as to the auditor's immediate client. The profession has always had to keep pace with developments on many fronts and I believe that it is well-qualified to meet the challenge of its new responsibilities. However, I argue strongly that the DTI must be more specific about the nature and the extent of the auditor's responsibilities to non-shareholders (that is, depositors and investors). The present proposals run the risk of creating an unsatisfactory open-ended responsibility which, in the present litigious environment, may result in a substantial increase in the risks of claims against auditors, and consequent insurance costs which would have to be passed on. I do not believe that this is the Government's intention, and so I would urge the DTI to set out any new responsibilities in more detail.

I can suggest a few areas where the auditor might be concerned about possible breaches of the SIB's (or SRO's) conduct of business rules. For example, the auditor may be able to 'protect the investor' by reporting to the supervisor on levels of investor protection:

1   advertising
2   client agreements
3   execution of transactions for clients
4   confirmation and accounts to clients
5   commissions and other charges
6   insurance and compensation fund arrangements
7   segregation of client money and investments
8   maintenance of adequate liquid capital.

Breaches of the last two examples will be the more black and white situations – but the auditor will still need to distinguish a range of situations extending from errors subsequently corrected to clear evidence of intended fraud. Higher up the list, the auditor may note instances of sharp practice as opposed to fraud and it will be more difficult to define the professional responsibilities of the auditor.

So, to summarise, it seems to me that there are three key issues arising from the DTI Consultative Document. Firstly, should auditors have the duty to report relevant information to the supervisor, or should they have the right? The consensus here seems to be moving towards a legal right, rather than a legal duty. Secondly, should auditors report information in any circumstances to the supervisor without informing the client? On this point, I believe that we have a professional duty (not a legal duty) to do so. But this professional duty must be backed up by adequate professional guidance. Thirdly, to what extent should the auditor take into account the interests of third parties – that is, those other than the shareholders of the client? I consider that the auditor must recognise that he has a special responsibility to depositors and investors, distinct from his traditional responsibility to shareholders.

The new regulatory framework raises important issues about the nature and the future role of the professional accountancy bodies. Many accountants will find that part of their business falls within the scope of 'investment business' as defined in the new legislation. These accountants will have to be authorised to carry on that investment business – authorised either by membership of a recognised professional body (RPB), or by the SIB/SRO routes. The professional bodies are considering whether they should seek to attain RPB status, which would involve introducing and monitoring a comprehensive set of rules that accountants would have to comply with when carring out investment business. The professional bodies may be wary of the administrative burden of setting up a comprehensive regulatory system for accountants who carry out investment business. However, the professional bodies may not wish to see other regulatory bodies (such as the SIB or the SROs) 'taking over' the role of exercising control over professional accountants. The accounting profession is going through a process of questioning what the professional bodies are there for – should the Institutes be like trade associations, with little regulatory control over members' activities? or should the Institutes accept the administrative burden of regulation, as being the price to pay of maintaining the authority and status of a self-regulatory profession?

The new regulatory framework also raises important issues about how auditors can be protected against possible litigation. The auditing profession is in an increasingly litigious environment, and we find that the availability insurance cover is contracting significantly. Insurance underwriters have identified the financial services sector as one in which the auditor is particularly at risk. Some audit firms are now refusing to take on work at the riskier end of the sector – that is, in precisely those cases where a high quality audit is most needed. The profession believes that auditors have an important role to play in the new regulatory framework. However, there is a danger that auditors will not be available to play this role, unless they are adequately protected against the potential open-ended liabilities that may arise if an investment business collapses. The profession believes that the solution to the problem lies in amending the Financial Services Bill so as to place a monetary limit on the liability of auditors of investment businesses. This limit might, for example, be some multiple of the audit fee, or it might be an absolute monetary amount. The key point is to ensure that the balance of risk and reward is not such as to deter auditors either from taking on investment businesses as clients, or from establishing a satisfactory relationship with the supervisory bodies.

Conclusion

I would like to end on a positive note by saying that I believe that the profession generally welcomes the new proposals in the financial services sector. The profession has always had to keep pace with developments on many fronts and I believe that the profession is willing and able to meet the challenge of its new responsibilities. There are a few important issues that are still to be resolved, but the profession is keen to demonstrate that it can make a significant contribution to the proposed new regulatory system.

The objective of the auditor must be to help ensure that his client has adequate reporting systems, internal controls, information systems, and that overall meets the needs of the SRO and the SIB. In 99 per cent of businesses this will probably be what clients want. It is only the 1 per cent that will try and avoid the responsibilities, and that is what we are all concerned about. Therefore, we must make certain that we build our controls and monitoring to catch the 1 per cent and not bog down the whole system in a welter of detailed reporting or monitoring. Indeed, that's what auditing is all about – to identify the key areas of control and ensure these are monitored and reported on. It is the exception to the rule which is crucial, more than producing a detailed mass of information.

7 A review of the legal problems

Professor R. B. Jack
of Glasgow University, McGrigor, Donald and Moncrieff and lay member of
The Stock Exchange

While the auditing profession may feel itself under pressure as the new
regulatory framework is put in place the legal profession is also faced with
new and perplexing problems. As Professor Jack points out, the emerging
financial conglomerates present a host of complex legal issues covering
the parent-subsidiary relationship, the regulation of multi-activity groups,
the obligations of principals towards clients, the disclosure of interests
and the role of 'Chinese Walls'. This lawyer's perspective on the Big Bang
inevitably raises more questions than it answers.

This section is based on two speeches by the Governor of the Bank of
England. In the first of those speeches given at a joint meeting of the
Glasgow Discussion Group on Finance and Investment and the
Edinburgh–Stirling Finance and Investment Seminar in the University of
Edinburgh on 6 March 1984 the Governor, under the title 'Changing
Boundaries in Financial Services', described the currents of change that
were eroding and, in some areas, sweeping away traditional barriers
between different types of financial services. In the second speech to The
Stock Exchange Northern Unit conference in Liverpool on 23 May 1984
the Governor reviewed developments in the securities market that
followed the announcement in July 1983 by the Secretary of State for
Trade of an agreement on the basis of which The Stock Exchange might
be removed from the ambit of the Restrictive Practices Court. These
speeches appear in the issues of the Bank of England Quarterly Bulletin
of March and June 1984.

   This section is concerned primarily with the legal aspects and
implications of some (at least) of the issues which have faced The Stock

Exchange and so have come before me in my capacity as a lay member of its Council. These issues were set out originally in The Stock Exchange's Discussion Paper of April 1984 from which flowed the Council's 'White Paper' on Membership and the Constitution issued in March 1985. It is considered that experience of The Stock Exchange will be reflected at least in essentials in other areas of financial activities.

I am writing from the perspective of a lawyer who has become quite closely involved with the affairs of one of the most important of our financial institutions: The Stock Exchange. The lay members of The Stock Exchange Council came to be appointed in particular circumstances. What had come to be known as the Case, that is the Director-General of Fair Trading's case against The Stock Exchange under the Restrictive Trade Practices Act had reached a crucial point and it was clear that the court was about to be asked to review a number of key features of The Stock Exchange among them fixed minimum commissions, single capacity (the separation of the functions of brokers and jobbers) and restrictions on outside shareholdings and participation in member companies. It was at this point, flushed with victory in the general election, that the Secretary of State for Trade announced to the House of Commons, on 27 June 1983, that the Government had decided that the rules and practices of The London Stock Exchange should be withdrawn from examination by the Restrictive Practices Court which is charged, under the Fair Trading Act, with examining restrictive practices and deciding whether they operate in the public interest.

The Secretary of State's statement set out the conditions which the Government had imposed for the removal of The Stock Exchange from the ambit of the Act. These conditions required that the Council should take action to dismantle by stages and with no unreasonable delay all the rules which prescribed minimum scales of commission, completing this by 31 December 1986. The Stock Exchange was to be permitted to continue the rules prescribing separation of capacity of brokers and jobbers, but was to be required to introduce rules to permit non-members to serve as non-executive directors of limited corporate members of The Stock Exchange, provided that there was always a majority of directors who were members of The Stock Exchange.

The condition, however, which brought me to the unfamiliar surroundings of the 22nd Floor of the Stock Exchange Tower was the introduction of lay members to the Council of The Stock Exchange. In addition to their other functions as members of the Council, it was made clear in the Secretary of State's announcement that the lay members were to play a special part in appeals against rejection of an application for membership and in the appeals element of The Stock Exchange's disciplinary procedures.

The Secretary of State concluded, 'I believe that these changes are to be welcomed and will enable The Stock Exchange to continue to adapt in an evolutionary manner to changing circumstances while maintaining proper regard for the needs and protection of investors'.

It was not surprising that the Director-General of Fair Trading was somewhat less than pleased at this settlement. In his Annual Report for 1983 he wrote:

> I cannot pretend that the Government's decision to relieve me of my duty to bring the case to court was not a blow to the Office. The views of a wide range of other financial institutions, industry and investors had been sought and much evidence was available to be deployed in the way of stock exchanges in New York, Toronto and elsewhere operated and how some of them had developed when similar restrictions had been removed. The court hearing due to begin in January 1984 would have brought out all the various public interest issues, the advantages of competition, the needs of investor protection, the imperatives of international competitiveness and so on. The court's considered judgement would have provided a highly informed basis for the future organisation of The Stock Exchange. . . . It has to be said, however, that by the end of 1983 it was clear that events had moved fast towards eliminating the very restrictions and practices which our litigation had challenged. The Stock Exchange agreed with the Government that it would give up minimum commissions by the end of 1986 and it became generally accepted that they would go, perhaps with a Big Bang, much earlier than that. Although single capacity was to remain, according to the agreement, for 'the time being', there emerged a general consensus that it would not, in practice, survive the end of minimum commissions. As for outside shareholdings, foreign and UK interests began to make purchases in brokers and jobbers with a clear eye to a not-too-distant future when The Stock Exchange itself would relax its current restrictions. By the year-end, we could console ourselves with the thought that more substantial changes were being brought about than the Government had required in July and that fixed commissions and other restrictions on competition may have persisted indefinitely but for our work of clarifying the issues for the impending scrutiny of those restrictions by the Restrictive Practices Court.

Since March 1986 100 per cent ownership of a member firm of The Stock Exchange by an outside organisation has been permitted and in the first week two new corporate members, Merrill Lynch from the USA and Nomura Securities from Japan, were admitted to membership. It has all been very exciting. I keep thinking of the Chinese curse 'May you live in interesting times'. As a lawyer, accustomed to looking for troubles and difficulties where perhaps none exist and to test the effectiveness of potential arrangements against such fundamental and starkly final changes of circumstances as death and liquidation. I would like to outline some of the issues which have concerned me as an observer from a legal perspective of the developments which have taken place and which are conveniently referred to as the City Revolution.

Issues arising from the Financial Services Bill

First, and by way of a preliminary, it is misleading in my view to refer to what is happening as 'deregulation'. What the Government has committed itself to doing in the Financial Services Bill currently before Parliament is to create a more far-reaching and universal system of regulation than has ever before operated in the United Kingdom in relation to investment business. Far from regulation becoming a thing of the past and the experience and skills of the regulator becoming as obsolete and obsolescent as those of a ship-builder, I anticipate that the demand in the City for regulatory and surveillance skills may soon become as great as that for market-makers and dealers. If Mrs Worthington is not to advise her daughter to go on the stage she might do worse than suggest that her daughter might become a compliance officer or the member of a surveillance department of a body which has aspirations to be recognised under the Bill (when it becomes an Act) as a self-regulating organisation.

What the Government is attempting to do in the Financial Services Bill is, of course, to encourage self-regulation within a statutory framework. This whole concept is one which our legislators, if the reports of the Parliamentary proceedings on the Bill are anything to go by, are having considerable difficulty coming to terms with. They are clearly haunted by the scandals at Lloyds – which of course is excluded from the Bill – at least pending the outcome of Sir Patrick Neill's investigation. (It is really a bit odd to title a Bill a Financial Services Bill when it not only excludes Lloyds but more importantly excludes our principal financial institutions in the shape of the banks at least in respect of their mainstream activities.) Be that as it may, our legislators are clearly concerned whether this hybrid of self-regulation within a statutory framework will be capable of achieving the measure of investor protection required to satisfy Professor Gower's criteria that it should 'protect reasonable people from being made fools of' and they are worried that troubles similar to those at Lloyds will emerge just as soon as Parliament has given us blessing to a system of control designed to avoid such abuses.

It is clear to me from the debates at the Committee Stage that Parliament is having difficulty in resolving the question of what is the proper balance of power between, on the one hand, a non-statutory body, to whom the powers of the Secretary of State are intended to be delegated without it becoming accountable to Parliament in the same way as a self-standing statutory commission and, on the other, those who are to be recognised as performing a regulatory role in particular areas of investment business (the SROs). The debate, as I read it, has centred on four issues. These are:

1   What powers is it legitimate to delegate to a non-statutory body without it becoming accountable to Parliament in the same way as a self-standing statutory commission?

2   The proper relationship of the designated agency (SIB) and the SROs particularly in regard to the rules of SROs.

3   The statutory powers and immunities required by SRO for the performance of their functions.

4   What role will the courts have in regulating the relationships between SIB and SROs?

In regard to these issues I make only four points. Firstly, as an advocate of the self-standing commission I do derive a little wry amusement from the fact that the number of dedicated advocates of self-regulation seem to have had a type of Damascus Road conversion to the statutory solution. Not wishing the pure white toga of self-regulation to be tainted in any way by governmental intervention they had haughtily (and in my view wrongly) rejected the Government's offer in its White Paper on Financial Services to give a measure of statutory support for the Take-Over Panel. They are clearly worried that the SIB (which we all assume will be the designated agency to which the Secretary of State will delegate his powers) will be able to achieve an acceptable measure of 'equivalence' (the level playing field) between the members of differing SROs. 'Equivalence' in relation to such matters as standards of investor protection and conduct of business is of course an essential element in the system of regulation proposed under the Bill and without it the members of The Stock Exchange as an existing SRO with a highly developed system of self-regulation see themselves at a competitive disadvantage with the members of the less mature, *nouveau* trade associations turned SROs. The worry arises from the belief that the volume of business which markets attract is an inverse function of the extent to which it is regulated. This is a view which is supported by the emergence of Panama and Liberia as 'great' maritime nations.

Secondly, I am old enough to remember the then Lord Chancellor, Lord Kilmuir, speaking in Glasgow about the problems of framing what he describes as, 'a justiciable issue', (by which he means an issue which the courts could reasonably be asked to determine) in the legislation which was then before Parliament and which represented the first attempt at scrutiny in the public interest of restrictive trade practices. I suspect that the courts may have to be the ultimate arbiters between the SIB and SROs particularly in regard to the content of their rules and so I wonder what question the courts are to be asked to determine. The courts are accustomed to dealing with such elusive concepts as 'fair and reasonable' and 'just and equitable' but what are the criteria by reference to which the courts are to decide whether, for example, a proposal by the SIB to impose a rule change on an SRO is appropriate?

Thirdly, the problem of immunity against legal action of SROs has become acute. The *Financial Times* of 24 April 1986 included an article headed, 'Big Bang Echoes may be heard in Court' which set out what it conceded was a hypothetical, over-simplified and perhaps exaggerated example which nevertheless illustrated one of the key issues facing the Government and the markets as the new regulatory structure takes shape.

The scenario envisaged in the article was as follows:

> The scene is the new City, after Big Bang and with a brand new self-regulatory system for London's securities markets. MegaGlobal Securities, a large US-based broker, is suspended for a week from trading in London by its UK self-regulatory organisation (SRO) – be it The Stock Exchange or one of five other projected SROs – for a breach of discipline. MegaGlobal, accustomed to the highly litigious atmosphere of the US, knows exactly what to do. It slaps a suit for wrongful suspension on the SRO and its executive officers claiming £100 million damages for lost business and defamation.
>
> The court finds that the SRO, though it had not acted out of malice, did not have sufficient grounds for suspending MegaGlobal. It awards the damages.
>
> Who is to pay? The SRO itself has few assets. Its executives clearly stand to be more than bankrupted. Even if the costs were spread out among all the SRO's members, the losses could still be substantial.
>
> Indeed, if there was a risk of such liabilities, many companies might not join SROs at all, instead registering directly with the Securities and Investments Board and effectively defeating the attempt to establish a system where the markets police themselves.
>
> No insurance company would be keen to take on the unquantifiable risks associated with claims such as MegaGlobal's. The SRO could go out of business. Its members could find that, in its absence, they have no authorisation to carry on their business.

There has come across my desk a Counsel's Opinion on the question of the liability of SROs under the Financial Services Bill. This makes it clear that these are the potential size of claims to which SROs could be exposed in the discharge of their functions are 'truly massive' and would be likely to inhibit SROs from effectively discharging these functions with the consequent risk of erosion of confidence of issuers and investors in the financial markets. Counsel conclude that there is no justification for a situation where the SIB will enjoy a wide statutory immunity while SROs have no immunity in the discharge of duties and functions imposed on them by statute.

The Chairman of The Stock Exchange is on the record as saying, 'I could not possibly recommend to the Council of The Stock Exchange that it seek to register as an SRO under the Financial Services Bill unless the Bill is amended to include appropriate immunity from suit for SROs'. The Government is currently examining the issue and deciding, as the *Financial Times* article said, whether it should group SROs under the Financial Services Bill with the Royal Society for the Prevention of Cruelty to Animals, as one of the very few private sector bodies granted this measure of statutory immunity.

Since this lecture was delivered the Secretary of State has announced (8 May 1986) that SROs are to be given immunity equivalent to that being conferred on the SIB. This immunity will extend to SROs, the members of their governing bodies and their officers and servants and will cover actions for damages for anything done or omitted in the discharge of the functions of the SRO unless the act or omission is shown to have been done in bad faith. It will not remove all legal remedies but only the right to claim damages. The right to sue for a declaration setting out the position on any legal issue in dispute will remain as also will the right to apply for an injunction (interdict) restraining an illegal act or requiring the SRO to act lawfully. The immunity will mean, however, that, provided the SRO acts in good faith, an investor who suffers loss as a result of an act or omission of an SRO will not be able to claim damages however seriously the SRO is at fault. It would seem likely, therefore, that as a *quid pro quo* the Government will require a higher level of compensation and professional indemnity insurance arrangements for SROs to protect those who may lose money as a result of the fraud or failure or even the negligence of their members.

Finally, of course, this whole question is but another aspect of the issue which the Wilson Committee on the Functioning of Financial Institutions described as being not 'whether statutory or non-statutory methods of supervision are preferable in some absolute sense, but whether the existing balance between the two, and equally, if not more importantly, the type of each presently used for the different groups of institutions, are appropriate for their particular circumstances'. Getting the balance right will not be easy.

As I indicated in my brief account of what has happened at The Stock Exchange since I became a lay member of its Council, the issues with which we have been concerned and the developments which have in fact taken place are related primarily to the question of who are to be permitted to play the game and what the rules are to be.

The players of the game

If I might begin with the players. In his speech in Edinburgh in March 1984 under the title of 'Changing Boundaries in Financial Services', the Governor gave his view that the partnership form of structure would increasingly give place to the corporate entity as the major form of business structure in the securities area. In support of that view, he said:

> In a securities trading structure in which firms are able to act as both agents and principals, a firm which wishes to operate in dual capacity role is likely to require a good deal more capital than is available to most partnerships. Indeed, to judge from American experience over the past decade or so, it seems quite likely that the partnership form will increasingly give place to the corporate entity as the major form of business structure in the securities area.

The partnership has traditionally been the form of business organisation adopted by providers of professional services. Apart from its tax effectiveness, partnership has over many years both before and after the Partnership Act of 1890 proved a most sensitive, adaptable and resilient form of business (and particularly professional practice) organisation. It has the advantage from the point of view of those dealing with it that it was based on the concept that those who owned it, not only managed it but were responsible for the whole of the extent of their wealth for any liabilities which it might incur. For the person relying on the intergrity as well as the professional knowledge and skill of the person with whom he is dealing there must be a comfort to be derived from the fact that the partner is backing with, not only his own wealth but that of all his partners, the standards of the work which he is doing for his client. The great threat to the solvency of most professional firms is not unprofitable trading but the unquantified liability flowing from the claims for negligence. We all of us wake up in the night thinking of the defective security, the undetected error in the accounts, the wrong diagnosis, the surgical instrument left inside the patient, the dry rot concealed below the immoveable wardrobe and the lost batch of British Telecom applications. We all have our own form of nightmare and we only get back to sleep when we remind ourselves of our professional indemnity insurance. It is, of course, the increasing difficulty of getting adequate indemnity insurance in the midst of the mega–claims being made against them that has stimulated the accountancy profession to seek a measure of limited liability, but clearly the Governor is right when he says that the partnership structure (even with the assistance of the special form of partnership introduced by the Limited Partnership Act of 1907 which provided for the limitation of liability for those partners not involved in the management and who wished simply to invest in the business) is not able to support the scale of business operations of those who wish to be major players in the future securities markets.

Even those who do not aspire to be major players and are content to continue to act as agency brokers have joined the flight from unlimited liability when they face the prospect of a potential collective liability as contributors, along with others who enjoy limited liability to a compensation fund to cover the defaults of their fellow members of an SRO. The move to limited liability company as the appropriate form of structure in the securities area has of course the advantage that (unlike the partnership structure) it requires the provision of fixed capital which can only be removed from the business in accordance with restrictions imposed to protect the interests of creditors. It does, however, give the regulators the problem of deciding what is an appropriate amount of fixed capital. When the Governor came again to Edinburgh at the beginning of 1985 and reviewed what was happening in the financial services field, he made the point that there could not be effective client protection unless all investment businesses were required to maintain net liquid assets sufficient to cover the threats to solvency posed by the principal risk which they face, for example, fluctuations in income, defaults by counter-parties and variations on the prices of investment in which the business holds positions.

And there have now come into force those provisions of the Insolvency Act 1985 which are designed to prevent the abuse of limited liability by imposing a much more strict regime for the disqualification of persons who have shown themselves unfit to be involved in the management of companies and for the personal liability of directors who have been found guilty of wrongful trading, a position which arises when a company goes on trading beyond the point when directors knew, or ought to be concluded, that there was no reasonable prospect that it would avoid going into insolvent liquidation unless at that stage they took every step with a view to minimising potential loss to the company's creditors as they ought to have taken. It will be an odd irony indeed if provisions directed at the fly-by-night travel agencies and mail order businesses strike home among the financial conglomerates and produce liability on the parent company for the debts and liabilities of the dealing subsidiary on the ground that the parent company is a 'shadow director' of the subsidiary in respect that the directors of the subsidiary are accustomed to act in accordance with its directions and instructions.

We have, of course, moved far from the mere incorporation of investment businesses into limited liability companies. A distinctive feature of the City Revolution has been the emergence of the financial conglomerate performing a multi-function role within the securities industry. This creates a real risk of cross-infection. It raises in a quite acute form how far a parent company and indeed other companies within the same group are responsible for the debts of a member of the group who gets into difficulties.

The Cork Committee, in reviewing what it called Group Trading in the sense of the conduct of various business by holding companies through a number of subsidiaries, concluded that it was not surprising that some of the basic principles of company and insolvency law fitted uneasily with the modern commercial realities of group enterprise and their report went on to quote what Lord Justice Templeman had said in his judgement (In re Southard & Co. [1979] 1 WLR 1198):

> English company law possesses some curious features which may generate curious results. A parent company may spawn a number of subsidiary companies, all controlled directly or indirectly by the shareholders of the parent company. If one of the subsidiary companies, to change the metaphor, turns out to be the runt of the litter and declines into insolvency to the dismay of its creditors, the parent company and the other subsidiary companies may prosper to the joy of the shareholders without any liability for the debts of the insolvent subsidiary.

This remains the law. The Cork Report made no suggestion for its alteration and the Insolvency Act does not change the position as stated in Lord Justice Templeman's judgement.

Of course, the position is confused rather than alleviated by cross guarantees within the group and I am sure it must be a real worry for the regulators who are charged with prudential supervision and regulation in the different areas of financial services.

My worry about cross-infection was increased rather than diminished by what Sir Martin Jacomb, the Vice Chairman of SIB, had to say in a paper delivered to the Royal Society of Arts in London in 1985. This is what he said:

> We must also ask ourselves what separate capitalisation of securities businesses owned by banks really achieves. It does make supervision easier. In particular, it makes it easier to ensure that businesses are not over-extending themselves, and that the same capital is not used to support two businesses. But is it really contemplated that a bank-owned separately capitalised securities subsidiary may go bust? We need to consider this. The typical well-managed US investment bank has capital which supports liabilities and assets of more than 20 times its size. It is obvious what risks this could entail if such a business was not well run. If such a business when owned by a bank runs into trouble, is it better for the bank to underwrite its losses and thus conceivably jeopardise confidence in the bank because it uses its capital in this way? Or is it better to allow the

subsidiary to fail, and preserve the integrity of the bank's capital but run the risk of loss of confidence because the bank had allowed its subsidiary to fail? These are fortunately theoretical questions at this stage, but we need to know how much faith we are really placing in separate capitalisation and why.

This is indeed a question to which regulators over the whole range of financial services will require to address themselves increasingly in the months ahead.

Having established that the players in the game are typically to be members of large (probably international) groupings of providers of financial services, the question which faces those who are charged with regulating their activities in any particular field is whether the participant is a 'fit and proper person' to be permitted to participate. The concept of the 'fit and proper person' is very much at the centre and core of the regulatory system as contained in the Financial Services Bill as it has been in the system of prudential supervision under the Banking Act 1979 and as it is intended to be in the system of building society supervision to be operated by the Building Societies Commission under the Building Societies Bill now before Parliament. At the very head of the require-ments for recognition of an SRO is that 'the rules and practices of the organisation must be such as to secure that its members are fit and proper persons to carry on investment business of the kind with which the organisation is concerned'.

It is trite to say that where the member is in fact a corporate body you have to look beyond him to the person who is in executive control of its business in order to determine fitness and propriety. I wonder how realistic that approach in fact is. I had occasion over the past few weeks to read the reports by the Department of Trade Inspectors appointed to investigate the affairs of a number of companies which were very much in the public eye (not always in a creditable way) in the 1970s. Reading these reports, one can hardly fail to appreciate that in many of the cases the troubles which beset the companies under investigation were clearly attributable to the 'dominant personality syndrome' where the dominant personality was the controlling shareholder who regarded the company and its assets as his own. Therefore I worry a little as to how in the crunch persons who have been recognised as 'fit and proper' will be able to resist the demands of their proprietors to do something which may be contrary to the spirit or even the letter of the rules and regulations of the SRO to which the company belongs. Strength of character and a willingness to put your career on the line must be part of the make-up of the 'fit and proper person' (as well as of those charged with surveillance, compliance and disciplinary functions) in the securities industry.

The Bank of England has, of course, had to face this problem in relation to its supervisory role under the Banking Act 1979. In their Annual Report for 1984 they wrote:

> With regard to a person who is a director, executive controller or manager of the institution itself, the Bank includes among the relevant considerations whether he has sufficient skills, knowledge, experience and application properly to undertake and fulfil his particular duties and responsibilities.
>
> In addition, the Bank takes into account the person's reputation and character, including such matters as whether he has a criminal record. In this connection the Bank is permitted by Section 43(2) of the Act to have regard to 'spent' convictions. Convictions for dishonesty are especially relevant, but the Bank also has regard to other types of offence since it is vital that a person responsible for managing a deposit-taking institution is of the highest integrity.
>
> In the case of existing license holders, the Bank has regard to the performance of the person in the exercise of his duties. Thus, imprudence in the conduct of an institution's business or anything which has threatened, without necessarily having damaged, the interests of existing or future depositors will reflect adversely on those responsible, whether the matters of concern have risen through the way they have acted or their failure to act in an appropriate manner.
>
> The Bank takes a 'cumulative' approach, so that it may determine that a person does not fulfil the criterion on the basis of several instances of such conduct which taken individually would not lead to that conclusion.
>
> The standards demanded are more onerous for those with prime responsibility for an institution's affairs, though they will vary according to the scale and nature of the business concerned. In all cases, the Bank looks for a firmly-based understanding of the institution's business and a clear conception of its future development, and also for evidence of sound judgement regarding both commercial and administrative matters relevant to the business.

This perhaps amplifies what the SIB have so far had to say in regard to what is required to satisfy the 'fit and proper person' test.

As I mentioned, the Secretary of State regarded one of the primary functions of lay members as being to ensure that The Stock Exchange did not refuse admission to those who were properly qualified to do so and I suspect that, increasingly, in implement of their requirement to secure that its members are fit and proper persons to carry on investment business, self regulating organisations will be faced with the difficult decisions as to when and in what circumstances it is legitimate for them to refuse admission to someone whose competence, experience, expertise may not be in doubt, but in relation to whom the question of 'fame and character' may raise its difficulties. How important an element is reputation or business standing. How legitimate are considerations which would lead to a 'black ball' in a club? Not all applicants have the capability for self-assessment and criticism of Groucho Marx.

In this connection I have read with some interest the Report issued recently of the Appeal Commissioner on the reference to him of an appeal against the decision of the Board of The London International Financial Futures Exchange (LIFFE) rejecting an application for membership. The application had been rejected because the LIFFE board had concluded that the applicant did not satisfy the criteria for membership set out in a rule of LIFFE which says that an applicant must satisfy the Board that he 'enjoys a financial and business standing suitable for a member of The Exchange.' The Board came to their conclusion, it was stated, primarily because of the large number of complaints which had arisen about the manner in which the applicant had dealt with its clients and because of media publicity adverse to the applicant. The Commissioner upheld the decision 'with some regret'. It was not, he said, in dispute that the applicant satisfied the financial and other criteria for membership of LIFFE. The matter turned on issues of judgement concerning reputation especially as to relationships with clients. He considered that the LIFFE Board were right to be concerned about the number of complaints which had been made about the applicant and he also accepted that the impact on the reputation of LIFFE, still a young organisation, of the admission to membership of the applicant, with the reputation which it had, was a legitimate consideration to be taken into account by the Board in considering the application. And he went on:

> This is not solely a matter of validity or otherwise of media comment on the applicant. Some of the comment may be tendentious or unfair or inadequately based in fact; but it is in itself a fact that the applicant has attracted significant adverse public comment. The reputation often out-lasts at least for a while, the factors which generate it. As of today I consider that the Board had grounds for concern about the reputation of the applicant.

And finally and interestingly, the Commissioner gave weight to what he described as a 'wider consideration'. This he described as the relationship of the appeal to the principles of the system being developed for the financial services industry of regulation within a statutory framework. In his view, the self-regulatory system requires that the considered judgement of the relevant practitioner body would normally be accepted and he accepted and supported it in the particular case before him.

It must be a matter for speculation, when and if the question requires to be considered by the courts, just how far they will consider it legitimate for an SRO, in considering whether an applicant is a fit and proper person for admission, to take into consideration adverse public comment (no matter how tendentious or unfair or inadequately based on fact) reflecting on the reputation of the applicant and in consequence his fitness for admission to the organisation.

The rules of the game

The SIB has now published its conduct of business rules and they are being subject to critical scrutiny and comment.

It is not my purpose here to join in the process. Suffice it to say that I have read a number of papers of considerable length and no doubt Sir Kenneth Berrill has read many more but my interest as a lawyer is really to test what is being done against the accepted fiduciary obligations of an agent because (at least in The Stock Exchange context) it is the departure from the dealing system based on separation of capacity which causes the most acute problems under the heading of 'conflicts of interest'. It may be true, as Sir Martin Jacomb suggests in his paper, that we have been rather too pre-occupied with conflicts of interest like the poor they have always been with us. Sir Martin instances as examples the conflict in fund management between the interests of the client and turnover-related remuneration; the conflict between a commission-paid insurance salesman and the interests of the purchaser; and the conflict between an issuer of securities and the investment funds under his discretionary management.

It is true, as Professor Gower said, that conflicts of interest have always been endemic in the securities industry and perhaps all that has happened now is that they have become more acute in the context of the abandonment of single capacity on The Stock Exchange and the emergence of the financial conglomerates. It is in this context that the traditional rules of the law of agency have assumed a new relevance. SIB have stated that their rules draw substantially on the law of agency. The law of agency is of course based on the premise that anyone charged with the management of the affairs of another must exercise the highest standards of skill and care and come under strict fiduciary duties in the performance of his functions. It is these fiduciary duties which are of particular concern since they require that the agent should not enter into any transaction in which his personal interest may conflict with his duties to his principal unless his principal consents. An agent must act in good faith with full disclosure of all material facts and not make secret profits. What the Governor described as 'the elegant solution' provided the single capacity system gave these protections by requiring the separation of the agency function of broking from the principal function of jobbing for most transactions and of course the SIB rules talk about the authorised person subordinating his own interests to those of his clients, acting fairly between his clients and disclosing the capacity in which enters into a transaction and interests in and facts material to the transaction. These all reflect the law of agency. That is all to the good but what does concern me is the increasing campaign from a number of areas for a modification of the strict rules of the law of agency on the ground that they are inconsistent with particular dealing systems and that clients will be sufficiently protected by a series of more detailed rules related to the suitability of investments for the particular client and imposing an obligation to execute clients' orders on the best available terms.

The SIB claims that its rules attempt to reconcile the fiduciary duty owed by a firm to its client with the fact that the firm or its associate may also be a principal market-maker in the investment concerned and they state that the effect is to require the firm to execute the transaction with another counter-party unless the client would receive at least as good a deal from the firm itself. In this way, it is considered, the fiduciary relationship and the obligations which it imposes on a person carrying on an investment business will survive the transformation of the relationship from an agent-principal basis to a principal-principal basis and so Professor Gower's dictum 'once an agent, always a fiduciary' will be observed. It goes, I am glad to say, beyond mere disclosure when Sir Martin Jacomb regarded it as 'the healthy answer' to 'conflicts of interest' on the grounds that 'if the client knows the facts he can make up his own mind' and 'if the conflict is literally unbearable, then commercial pressure will make that method of doing business impossible.'

What worries me in all this is whether what is being provided will maintain the trust and confidence which the law of agency in its wisdom saw as essential to the relationship between principal and agent. If I might illustrate by one simple and obvious example. Under the new regime, the private client who goes to his broker (as he will still regard him) to consider and seek advice on a possible sale of his holdings in ICI or even a possible purchase of shares in ICI, will, under the new regime, be likely to be met with his broker reminding him that as he is a market-maker in this particular stock he may ultimately suggest that the transaction be done with him as a principal rather than through him as an agent. In my view that completely alters the relationship between the parties which no amount of disclosure or best execution can ever fully restore. The advice in my view becomes tainted and the suspicion naturally arises as to how far the broker-dealer will truly 'subordinate his own interests to those of his client'. The appearances are important. There must not only be, but be seen to be, good faith and fair dealing. I welcome the SIB's view that it will expect all firms to treat all customers as clients (with all the fiduciary obligations which that relationship carries) unless there is a clear understanding on both sides that a different relationship subsists. But I would like to think that we might go further than that and require a firm to decline to act in all cases where the circumstances are such that the conflict makes it impossible for the firm to transact business with or for a client in the best interests of the client, or to give objective and independent advice to the client on a prospective transaction.

I have a nagging doubt as to whether adequate thought has been given to the detrimental effects on the capacity of an investment adviser to protect the interests of a particular client where he is part of an organisation which operates effective Chinese Walls. Investment, it is trite to say, is based on information. Chinese Walls are, of course, directed at the restriction of the passage of information but I wonder whether the clients will always appreciate the effect of his individual interests of restrictions on the passage of information. For example, a Chinese Wall between the corporate finance department and the investment department may prevent investment advisers and fund managers from making investment decisions or giving advice based on a genuine assessment of the performance of a particular company when they know, as they must, that that particular company is a corporate finance client of the group and when they suspect that the corporate finance department has information which confirms the hunch on which he would otherwise have given his investment advice or made his investment decision. And generally investment advisers and fund managers would be less than human if they did not tend to be much more cautious and circumspect about investment in concerns which had a client relationship with their own organisation. A stop list is the most acute example of a circumstance in which an investment adviser or fund manager will be prevented from taking steps to protect and improve his client's position in relation to a security which is the subject of a stop. Will clients fully appreciate and accept this real restriction on the value of the investment advice which they are receiving, or the investment decisions made on their behalf?

8 The American experience: bank supervision in the United States

L. William Seidman

Chairman, Federal Deposit Insurance Corporation, Washington, DC

Whereas UK financial deregulation is coming all at once, the US experience has been much more gradual. There is, therefore, something to be learned from the results of US deregulation to date. In this concluding paper William Seidman points to some of the risks associated with deregulation and the accompanying need for intensified supervision. At the top of the US regulators' agenda for reform are proposals, considered here, for refining capital adequacy assessments and for establishing a risk-based deposit insurance system.

What better vantage point could a US bank supervisor choose for contemplating the new wave of competition in his own country's financial services industry than the exciting deregulatory scene dramatically unfolding in the United Kingdom?

I am particularly encouraged to see a handful of US banks positioning themselves as active competitors in the British market. The dismantling of all restrictions against ownership of stock exchange firms in March 1986 and the anticipated elimination of barriers between securities dealers and underwriters should reshape the British financial services sector. The fortuitous circumstances of having a few US banks participating in the British experience is going to focus attention on how well American bank managers can handle the risks of new products and delivery systems. This is going to give US supervisors a jump on the situation and make them better prepared for the widespread deregulation that is bound to take hold eventually in the States.

I feel confident that in due time the United States will take steps comparable to the far reaching deregulatory initiatives adopted in the

United Kingdom. This will present greater challenges to the ability of supervisors to measure risk and maintain the safety and soundness of the financial system. In the light of these challenges, I would like to explain some aspects of US bank supervision, describe major changes we are making in the supervisory process, and note some of the major issues that must still be resolved.

Historical background

To put the supervisory challenge in proper perspective, a short lesson in modern American banking industry is in order. Let me start in the Roaring Twenties, when American bankers were a rather freewheeling lot. Banks offered a variety of financial products, underwrote securities and participated in business ventures. They had a substantial amount of discretion to price their products as they saw fit.

Banks also had substantial authority to operate where they wished. State chartering agencies' geographic restrictions on the scope of in-state bank operations did not apply to federally-chartered banks. Moreover, banking entrepreneurs operated across state lines by establishing holding companies. Banks were, of course, subject to safety and soundness regulations and supervision. But, to a significant degree, they were free to carry on their affairs as they saw fit.

Then came the Crash of Twenty-Nine, followed in short order by waves of bankruptcies and the collapse of numerous banks. Congressional inquisitors sought out villains to blame for this sorry turn of events and bankers served as ready scapegoats. Bankers, it was said, had 'sinned' by entangling themselves in the hurly-burly of commerce, by 'pumping up' worthless stock for a quick profit and by abandoning sound lending practices.

Telling bankers to 'sin no more' was not enough; Congress decreed that banks had to be removed from all sources of temptation. Accordingly, the Banking Act of 1933 enforced a separation of banking from commerce and largely prohibited bank underwriting activities. The products banks could offer – and the prices they could set – came under federal regulation. A new law subjecting federally-chartered banks to state geographic restrictions was strictly enforced. A Federal Deposit Insurance Corporation – the FDIC – was created, charged with paying off all small depositors of failed banks. That institution, funded through annual assessments on member banks, was able to stem the tide of bank runs and restore stability to the banking system. This self-serving assessment was made not by me, but by those philosophical antagonists, Milton Friedman and John Kenneth Galbraith.

While federal deposit insurance clearly was a valuable step forward,

some economic historians have questioned the need for the other
Depression era restrictions. Those scholars have argued that the 'sins' of
which banks were accused were blown out of proportion, and were not
responsible for the 1930s' economic collapse. Whether accurate or not,
those observations are merely academic. The fact is that that Gulliver of
the American economy, the banking system, became ensnared in a
multilayered regulatory web. Like good Lilliputians, the regulators wove
new regulatory strands whenever Gulliver flexed his muscles. For
example, when banks started to evade geographic restrictions on
banking through holding company acquisitions. Congress quickly
passed the Bank Holding Company Act of 1956. That law gave individual states veto powers over out-of-state holding company acquisitions.
Because almost all states prohibited such acquisitions, interstate banking
soon became a dead letter. When banking holding companies threatened
to expand their range of product offerings, the law was amended,
allowing the Federal Reserve Board to disallow activities deemed 'not
closely related' to banking.

The message is clear: Congress created the chains that bound the
banking industry, and government regulators made sure they stayed in
place; regulators told banks where they could operate, what products
they could offer and what prices they could charge. The aim of such tight
'command and control' supervision was, in effect, to 'lull banks to sleep'.
Bankers were to lead quiet lives and not enmesh themselves in the
rough-and-tumble world of the commercial marketplace. Risk-taking
that could disturb the system was to be avoided at all costs. Like the
puritan divine who worried that 'somehow, somewhere, someone
might be enjoying himself', regulatory officials lived in constant fear that
competition might break out – a dire result to be avoided at all costs.

For many years the system puttered along smoothly. Three supervisory barons – the Comptroller of the Currency, the Federal Reserve
Board and the FDIC – controlled their separate domains. The Comptroller told federally-chartered banks what to do. The Federal Reserve Board
regulated bank holding companies and state-chartered bank members of
the Federal Reserve System – that is, banks that chose to avail themselves
of certain Federal Reserve System facilities. The FDIC held sway over
state non-member banks. This compartmentalised system – which arose
by historical accident, not design – worked surprisingly well, despite a
lack of co-ordination among the three federal barons.

The prototypical banker was the 'organisation man' in the grey flannel
suit, content to live quietly and do what he was told. Not all bankers fit
that mould, of course. The more entrepreneurial sorts lived 'lives of quiet
desperation', eager to innovate but prevented from doing so by federal
and state watchdogs.

Eventually, however, the system began to crumble at the edges. What man had created, market forces eroded. Non-bank financial service firms began offering bank-like products accessible to small depositors, such as money market mutual funds. Businesses not regulated under the banking laws began marketing bank-related services to their customers through 'one-stop-shopping' financial supermarkets. New technologies, such as electronic fund transfers, helped this process along. So did clever lawyers, who exploited legal loopholes to create 'non-bank banks' and other exotic, less-than-fully regulated entities.

The non-bank bank is a strange beast that arose in recent years, created by securities firms and other businesses that wanted to enter the banking business. They took advantage of the fact that federal law defines a nationally-chartered bank as an organisation that both takes deposits and makes loans. The 'non-bank' does not make loans but does take deposits – deposits that are insured by the FDIC. In January 1986 the US Supreme Court struck down the Federal Reserve Board's attempt to close the non-bank loophole by regulatory redefinition. Thus, the non-bank – which can avoid geographic restrictions that apply to 'bank banks' – will continue to thrive, unless and until new legislation renders it extinct.

The non-bank bank was only one of many devices businesses employed to poach on the bankers' domain. The banks were bound to react, and they did. To hold their customers, they began experimenting with new products, expanding their interstate activities and testing the limits of the prohibitions against underwriting. Although they initially resisted this shocking outbreak of competition, Congress and federal regulators in recent years began to give way, at least at the margins. They realised that if banks were to remain viable competitors, they simply had to be given greater pricing and operational flexibility. New laws and regulatory modifications have begun dismantling command and control restrictions on bank activities.

This has fostered a financial marketplace more responsive to consumer needs. I must admit, however, that we have only advanced a few tentative steps down the deregulatory road. Interest rate ceilings and other restrictions on the prices banks can charge for their offerings have been abolished. A greater amount of interstate activity is permitted. We are allowing banks to offer a somewhat more varied menu of financial products, such as discount brokerage services. Nevertheless, we are still far from a regime of full-scale interstate banking. Restrictions on interstate holding company acquisitions – except when the acquired bank is failing – remain in place. Similarly, numerous state law limitations on interstate mobility – and on geographic diversification within states – remain on the books. Furthermore, banks are still largely barred from corporate underwriting and other 'commercial' functions.

Legislative proposals to loosen some of these regulatory bonds are under consideration. For example, the Reagan administration supports a measure that would allow banks to underwrite commercial paper. But old Washington hands like myself do not expect an overnight transformation of the system, akin to what is happening in the United Kingdom. In the American banking landscape, the canvas of change features minute, carefully crafted etchings, rather than sweeping, broad brushstrokes.

This reluctance to embrace rapid change renders some observers indignant. They attribute legislative inaction to the connivance of investment firms that scheme to keep commercial banks from poaching on their turf. Certainly, there is a hollow ring to the bleatings of those poor sheep who would keep commercial bankers out of the investment field – but who reserve the right to steal away traditional banks' customers. Claims that new bank powers threaten conflicts of interest, financial instability, and unspecified 'subtle hazards' to business as usual also appear rather suspect. The risks of securities underwriting are manageable and of short duration – and lower than with many types of commercial lending. Securities law information disclosure requirements and bank law controls on insider transactions enable the market to monitor and discipline self-dealing. Our central bank, the Federal Reserve Board, is much better able to deal with monetary contraction and related financial instability than in the 1920s or 1930s.

Dr Pangloss might say, 'Aha! The arguments against deregulation are utter drivel. Everything is for the best in this best of all possible worlds. Let us fully deregulate at once.' I, however, am a conservative, Burkean to the core. I worry. I am instantly suspicious when told that a system that has facilitated America's rapid economic growth in these last 50 years – with scarcely a hitch, mind you – runs no risks from massive free market surgery. If surgery is called for – and I believe it is – a trained physician had better monitor the patient's convalescence.

That Scottish apostle of free markets, Adam Smith, warned in *The Wealth of Nations* about the perils to commerce and industry arising from 'the unskillfulness of the conductors of paper money'. Surely this concern is as valid in the twentieth century as it was in the eighteenth. Indeed, the mischief caused by banks' 'unskillfulness' – and, I would add, 'unscrupulousness' – is magnified by the new opportunities deregulation creates. In short, deregulation poses an increased challenge for that policeman of the banking world, the bank supervisor.

Challenge to bank supervision

The move from a regulated to a deregulated banking environment bears a striking resemblance to the move from a police state to a free society. In a police state, the citizenry is cowed, making it relatively easy to keep a lid on violent crime. Unfortunately, a police state also prevents individuals from speaking up in public, and puts a crimp on merrymaking. Similarly, bankers were cowed in the days of heavy regulation. Outright fraud and theft were certainly reined in, but so were procompetitive product line and geographic diversification – the banking counterparts of free speech and merrymaking.

Now observe what happens when police state controls are lifted. Individuals are able to express themselves freely in public, and welfare rises – much as consumers and businesses benefit from new products and services following bank deregulation. But at the same time, the policeman's job becomes harder. Violent criminals find it easier to circulate in public, and even 'average citizens' may have fewer inhibitions. 'Making merry' may lead to accidents behind the wheel, injuring innocent bystanders. Thus, in a free society, the policeman is transformed from a regulator into a supervisor. He must allow free speech and public merriment, but be ready to step in when liberty becomes unrestrained license. While this job may be relatively less demanding in more 'civilized' societies where the public order is widely respected, it presents a significant challenge in all democratic nations. Bank supervisors increasingly will face the same problem. They must allow banks to compete in new areas, while keeping a sharp eye out for trouble – whether by hard core embezzlers and corporate looters, or by 'solid citizens' who drink too freely of the wine of risky opportunities. These policing functions are particularly hard to carry out in the United States, which in 1985 boasted a grand total of 14,405 federally-insured commercial banks. Obviously, the possibilities for fraudulent and excessively risky behaviour are manifold in a society with so many banking institutions.

In order further to clarify the distinction between regulation and supervision, I would commend to you the example of the American airline industry. I happened to be in the Ford White House when the blueprint for airline deregulation was laid out. The plan was to eliminate economic regulations that fixed airline prices and routings, while leaving safety supervision in place. That plan has been implemented and airlines are free to enter and exit geographic markets, charging the prices they choose. On the whole, passengers have certainly benefited. Airline bankruptcies have also soared, as the market has weeded out ineffective competitors. And, while airline travel safety remains high, safety supervisors have their hands full. They have to watch out that aggressive competitors, living on reduced margins, do not excessively 'cut corners' on maintenance and crew training in order to stay in business. Those worries were far less serious in the old days of the US airline cartel, when everyone had his share of the pie and price competition did not matter.

Now let us take a closer look at American banks. How have they fared lately? The short answer is, not too well – or at least not as well as they have historically. Average banking earnings and profitability have fallen in the last few years – both absolutely and relative to the risks banks assume. The return on average assets for all banks has declined steadily, falling from .82 per cent in 1980 to .64 per cent in 1985. The percentage of banks with a good return on assets – over 1 per cent – has also fallen precipitously, from 60.47 per cent in 1980 to 43.14 per cent in 1985. Bank failures have also mounted, from 42 in 1982, 48 in 1983, 79 in 1984, to 120 in 1985. This compares most unfavourably to the average of about ten a year in the 1970s.

A small chart, which follows below, summarises recent key performance indicators for all insured commercial banks:

	1980	1981	1982	1983	1984	1985
Return on Average Assets	.82%	.81%	.74%	.67%	.65%	.64%
Per cent of banks with good return on assets (over 1%)	60.47%	56.56%	53.07%	48.14%	43.03%	43.14%
Per cent of banks with negative return on assets (under 0%)	3.71%	5.14%	8.33%	10.99%	13.82%	16.16%
Net charge-offs as a percentage of average total loans	.38%	.37%	.57%	.69%	.78%	.86%
Loss reserves as a percentage of average total loans	1.06%	1.10%	1.15%	1.26%	1.35%	1.51%

However, it would be wrong to be too over-pessimistic. Without deregulation, banks would have experienced a massive outflow of funds to non-bank financial institutions and suffered a tremendous erosion in their competitive health. Deregulation was the tonic that banks needed to avoid serious illness. Already that tonic has produced significant benefits: it has helped weed out ineffective management; it has allowed economies of scope from complementary financial activities to be realised and it has enabled consumers and producers to enjoy new products and services and to take advantage of 'one stop shopping' opportunities. In short, bank deregulation has been a marvellous success story.

Of course, competition sharpens as regulatory obstacles are removed. In order to compete effectively, many banks will take larger risks – and some of those institutions are bound to incur losses. The lifting of interest-rate ceilings eliminates cheap deposits. Aggressive banks, in order to pump up liquidity, will pay premium rates for fully-insured brokered deposits sold in $100,000 blocs. This 'hot' money can appear and then disappear literally overnight – hastening a bank's demise. Speculative loans may be needed to pay the premium for brokered funds. If those loans sour, a weak bank will swiftly collapse.

Deposit insurance compounds the incentive to take excess risks in a deregulated environment. It does this by interfering with the free market's ability to price the cost of a bank's funds as a function of the risk that the bank incurs. In order to counteract this, we have explored the possibility of co-insurance – similar to the system in the UK – whereby depositors would be paid only 75 or some other percentage of their insured deposits in the event of failure. We also considered the possibility of placing the uninsured deposits – amounts in excess of the $100,000 limit of insurance per account – at greater risk.

Neither possibility, however, seems politically feasible at this time. Our experience with the Continental Illinois Bank rescue, where we arranged an assistance package that had the effect of *de facto* 100 per cent deposit insurance, should tell us that we do not have the tools to pay off a giant bank or to assess properly the potential systemic harm of such a pay off. As a consequence, and to prevent the flight of large deposits from small banks to the largest, we should be thinking along the lines of providing 100 per cent deposit insurance without regard to any limit per account. In some cases, we have it *de facto*; the question is, should we have it *de jure*?

And should deposit insurance be limited to transactions accounts – accounts that can be withdrawn without notice? Consider holders of certificates of deposit over $100,000, letters of credit and other off balance-sheet guarantees and additional bank liabilities. Should they be put on clear legal notice that their funds will not be guaranteed by the FDIC? If this limitation is put in place, we would need some means of keeping opportunistic bankers from sweeping as much as they could under the deposit insurance umbrella.

Given the realities of *de facto* deposit insurance, we must recognise that the deposit insurance agencies and the government, where it is the *de facto* insurer of deposit accounts, are subject to a considerable moral hazard. While most bankers are competent and honest and manage their banks prudently and efficiently, there are some who are not. Some bankers are willing to take great risks in the hope of making a fortune and a few are crooks. Deposit insurance largely removes the necessity for depositors to monitor how banks are operated.

Nor are restrictions on how a bank can be run – what assets it can hold, which services it can offer, where it can branch, and how it should structure its liabilities – an adequate response to the situation. Such restrictions would unacceptably cripple banks' ability to compete with non-bank financial service firms. Moreover, bankers who want to take risks have ample means of doing so in today's marketplace. They can hold long-term fixed interest rate securities that are funded with short-term liabilities and hope that interest rates fall. Or they can do the reverse and hope that interest rates rise. Or they can buy and sell interest rate futures and options contracts. They can make risky loans for high fees and interest rates or equity participations. There is almost no end to the ways in which the determined risk-seeking banker can gamble with, in effect, the FDIC's funds. The thieves can make self-dealing and outright fraudulent loans, as they have throughout history. With FDIC-insured depositors not very concerned, smarter and more vigilant supervision is essential.

The supervisor's increasing difficulty in controlling risk and maintaining safety and soundness in the system can now be appreciated. As banks get into a wider range of activities and as bankers become less conservative, the supervisors must increase their knowledge and oversight. Thus deregulation must be balanced with intensified supervision. Elimination of broad-brush rules that apply to all banks must be offset with aggressive case-by-case action to deal with individual problem banks.

The trouble is that developing and implementing new supervisory initiatives to address the risks and vulnerabilities of a deregulated environment is not easy. Regulators continually face the task of steering a course between what is good for the individual institution and what is good for the system. At the same time we must sort out the risks inherent in the changing operations of both the institutions and the marketplace. The FDIC has tried to meet these new challenges by reviewing and streamlining our internal operating procedures and by adopting policies that shift the focus of our efforts toward ensuring that the banks themselves are prepared to manage these new risks.

Supervisory initiatives

At the operating level, an insurance organisation must have an effective risk identification and control system to limit losses. In the case of the FDIC, these preventative steps take on increased importance, because of the potential disruption that can result from a bank failure. The need for rapid action has been intensified by the advent of computers, combined with the increase in 1980 of deposit insurance from $40,000 to $100,000 per account. Now a bank can obtain a very large amount of funds very quickly, either through its own efforts or through brokers, from depositors who have no economic reasons to be concerned with the safety of the bank or with how it intends to use the funds. Thus a risk-taking or crooked banker can subject the FDIC to great losses in a very short time.

Bank examination

Historically, the bank examination process has been the heart of the FDIC's risk identification programme. Not so very long ago on-site examinations were conducted at frequent intervals on all institutions under our direct supervision. Their purpose is to:

1   provide an analysis of a bank's financial condition
2   appraise the quality of bank management, including the board of directors
3   identify areas where corrective action may be necessary
4   determine overall compliance with applicable laws and regulations.

We still are trying to achieve those objectives, but the procedures for doing so have changed drastically.

We have moved away from the static, point-in-time reviews to more dynamic, continuous supervision. We have lengthened our examination cycles for the well-run banks in order to concentrate our limited resources on those institutions that present the greatest exposure and risk of failure. It is better to revisit a problem bank a second or third time than to visit a satisfactory bank once. This has been possible because we have developed sophisticated off-site computer monitoring systems and have increasingly relied on a number of state banking departments for day-to-day supervision of many well-run banks.

Through automatic screening techniques, off-site monitoring helps target specific banks for on-site review and identifies areas within those banks that show symptoms of emerging problems. Furthermore, it allows us to keep track of changes in the way banks are run so that we can move into situations for which our past favourite experience may no longer be relevant.

Automation is also playing a larger role in our on-site examination programme. Today's examiners are much better equipped than their predecessors to evaluate a bank's condition. By using portable computers they have instant access to a wealth of bank performance and peer group data stored on our central database. Some loan analysis is being done with computers. We are developing sophisticated computer models and forecasting techniques to improve further on-site analysis. Furthermore, examiners now have the capability to transmit their findings electronically on an automated report format back to their regional offices.

Because of resource limitations, we have placed more emphasis on planning the examinations and targeting our resources to those areas of the bank that exhibit the greatest risk potential. One area we expect to stress is the bank's internal control systems. While our examiners have always reviewed this area, the increasing importance of sound control systems for the prevention of fraud and insider abuse warrants greater examiner attention. We expect to use more statistical sampling procedures to detect deficiencies and then use stringent follow-ups to determine if the control deficiencies were corrected. We are even evaluating the possibility of having the banks outside CPAs play a greater role in our examination process. Our goal for the future is to identify and use effectively all available supervisory tools, whether they are in the public or private sector.

Evaluating credit risk is still a major part of our examination programme and it will continue to be. But we will highlight portfolio diversification more than ever before. The problems we have seen in banks serving the American agricultural and energy sectors demonstrate why diversification is so important.

When problems are encountered at an on-site examination, our function is not to manage the bank. Rather, it is to work with management and the bank's board of directors to correct weaknesses and limit exposure to risk. If this proves unsuccessful, we have authority to impose enforcement actions, the procedures for which have been recently streamlined. The severity of those actions depends on the severity of the problem. Actions can range from simple agreements for correcting minor deficiencies or problems to cease and desist orders. Those orders may require the removal of bank officers, civil money penalities and, ultimately, the elimination of deposit insurance coverage.

Inter-agency co-operation

But even with all these changes to our examination and supervisory programmes, much more needs to be done. The multi-tiered financial services industry that evolved out of the 1930s was monitored by a similarly complex regulatory apparatus. Co-ordination was not a major concern of the regulators. But times have changed. If deregulation has proved anything, it has proved that co-operation between regulators is essential. It has also shown that such co-operation should extend to the private sector and to the public at large. No longer do regulators have the luxury of concerning themselves solely with institutions under their direct supervision. In today's environment, co-operation is the name of the game.

I have already mentioned that the FDIC depends on many state banking departments to shoulder more of the burden for on-site examinations of well-run institutions. The FDIC simply does not have the resources to cover the increasing number of banks requiring special supervisory attention without some assistance with the well-run institutions. But this co-operative effort is not a one-way street. In return we are providing the states with training, legal assistance, examination forms and access to our computer database.

At the federal level, co-operation has been and will continue to be one of our top goals. We have initiated co-operative examination pro-grammes for multibank holding companies exhibiting a high risk profile and for the multinational institutions whose size alone makes them a high potential risk to the FDIC. We have also implemented policies for sharing confidential supervisory information between bank and thrift supervisors. These efforts recognise that prompt and effective communi-cation among the supervisors is in the best interest of all concerned, if excessive risks and abuses within the financial services industry are to be contained.

Since I have become Chairman of the FDIC, co-operation between the agencies has even extended to the breakfast table. Federal Reserve Chairman Paul Volcker, Comptroller of the Currency Robert Clarke and I try to maintain regularly-scheduled breakfast meetings to discuss regulatory and supervisory issues. I believe these meetings have been quite beneficial. I certainly see a co-operative spirit developing among the agencies.

This brings me to my final point about co-operation. The spirit of co-operation among supervisors has not stopped at national borders. The interdependence of world markets has necessitated more harmoni-sation and co-operation to tighten the supervision of multinational banks. We have come a long way in the past few years and I am hopeful that these efforts will continue.

Problems of geographic and product line diversification

Increased co-operation among banking supervisors has come just in the nick of time. Such co-operation will be needed to confront emerging challenges posed by geographic and product line diversification.

First, let us focus on geographic diversification. As geographic barriers continue to erode, the emerging interstate banking environment will pose new supervisory problems for the regulators. Regional interstate banking compacts among neighbouring states currently appear to be a reasonable first step toward nationwide banking. How this will eventually turn out we do not know, although some form of nationwide banking seems inevitable. What we do know, however, is that our present supervision programme is inadequate for the task. An effective interstate examination and supervision programme that co-ordinates the resources of all affected regulators is a necessity.

Product line diversification is blurring the traditional distinctions among lines of commerce. The forces of the marketplace are making the wall between banking and commerce more porous each day. While there are sharp restrictions as to what types of business organisations may own banks, there are no such restrictions on the types of businesses that individuals who own banks may engage in. The result is that we have real estate developers, car dealers, insurance agents and others, from all walks of life, owning and operating banks. The only restriction is that they are prohibited from placing the bank and other business interests under one corporate umbrella.

Over the years the FDIC has permitted a number of non-bank firms to acquire limited service banks. The FDIC also insures numerous industrial banks that are owned by many types of financial enterprises. The key question being asked is, how do you supervise these business entities as well as bank holding companies that are also diversifying into non-traditional banking activities? Should the entire organisation come under close scrutiny even when the bank is only a small part? Or should a supervisory bubble be placed over the bank to try to ensure that the resources of the bank are not tapped to support an affiliate company? Should non-bank activities be conducted within the bank, as part of a separately funded affiliate of the bank, or in a holding company structure? Will the operating efficiencies lost by adding corporate layers be sufficiently offset by the added insulation to the bank? While we in the US are still debating these questions, I have noted with great interest the recent policy notice issued by the Bank of England on this very issue. I believe that UK research in this area will be quite helpful to the United States.

Bank capital policy

Outside the internal operations area, the FDIC has adopted, or is considering adopting, bank capital and risk-related deposit insurance policies designed to enhance our supervisory capabilities. I will turn first to bank capital. Few disagree with the importance of adequate capital during times of economic uncertainty and change. The challenge supervisors face is how to set capital requirements effectively and fairly.

The first problem facing a capital standard is how to measure capital. We would like the standard to refer to economic capital rather than to an accounting number equalling the difference between book assets and book liabilities. Banks' and other enterprises' accounting statements are designed primarily for purposes of control, not as measures of economic market values. For example, many important assets are understated or not recorded at all on a bank's books.

Some examples are customer goodwill, employee training and loyalty, buildings and equipment purchased at times when price levels were lower, and systems development and computer software. Other assets often are overstated. These include loans to countries carried at face value even though the borrower's ability to repay is in doubt, and fixed-interest obligations carried at cost even though subsequent interest rate increases have reduced their present values. Long-term fixed-interest liabilities can be similarly overstated. Considerable research is required before we could implement market-value accounting or even substantially improve our current historical-cost accounting for capital.

A second problem is the standard to be applied. How much capital is enough? How much is too much? In 1985 the US federal bank regulators finally agreed on a uniform capital ratio for commercial banks of 6 per cent of balance sheet assets. This was no mean accomplishment, since the agencies had debated the issue for years. Initially we were quite pleased with the industry's reaction, as many banks took quick steps to bolster their capital. However, as we all know, there are a variety of methods to increase capital ratios – some more desirable than others. Banks can increase their accounting-measured capital in ways that do not reduce the risk to the deposit insurance agencies. For example, banks can and have sold their buildings and leased them back. If they are only realising the capital gains they had but were unable to record, the result is that their balance sheets better reflect their economic condition. This better accounting comes at the price of transactions' costs such as real estate agents' fees and transfer taxes and higher income taxes. However, the sale and lease back can be structured to overstate the bank's capital. Since the purchasers of the building would be willing to pay the present value of the lease payment, the sale price of the building and hence the bank's capital could be increased by the simple expedient of specifying a high promised lease payment. The bank's economic capital is not higher, because it has an unrecorded liability to pay the higher lease amounts. But the bank's accounting capital is greater.

Another rather simple method to boost bank capital is through selective selling of fixed-interest rate obligations. Those with unrecorded capital gains are sold while those with unrecorded capital losses are held.

Perhaps a more serious problem is the tendency of banks to increase their risk exposure with off-balance sheet activities. Rather than take in a deposit and make a loan, a bank might guarantee a loan from one customer to another for a fee. Had it gone the first route, the bank's capital ratio would be lower. By shifting to off-balance sheet activities, the bank reduces its recorded assets and liabilities, thereby increasing the ratio of its capital to assets. But the riskiness of its activities and its need for capital has not decreased.

The entire issue of off-balance sheet activity is an excellent example of the supervisory challenges of a deregulated environment. The volume and diversity of this activity has grown to such an extent that we are now seeking ways to factor the risk into our capital calculation. Here again I am grateful to the Bank of England for providing us with the results of their analysis on off-balance sheet risk.

In view of the growing complexities of assessing risk, we are looking at other ways to relate capital to the risk undertaken. Gaining widespread notoriety, if not widespread support, have been some recent proposals for risk-based capital. Each of the federal agencies has issued preliminary proposals for public comment. As these comments are received, we will undertake analysis aimed at developing a uniform program that is acceptable to our banks and to all the US bank regulators.

One stated reason for the proposal was to move towards a convergence of international standards for measuring capital adequacy. An international standard for capital would be most welcome, since it is difficult to make valid comparisons when every country counts it differently. We should recognise, however, that comparisons among countries and even among banks in a single country are limited by divergences between accounting and economic measures of assets and liabilities.

While we are trying to develop more meaningful measures for bank capital, we also have had to make our present capital standards somewhat flexible. As I have already explained, severe problems afflicting farm and energy production have strained the banks that service those sectors. Responding to this problem, we regulators have agreed to adopt a capital forbearance policy that allows those affected banks to operate temporarily with lower capital ratios if they meet certain requirements. This is a controversial initiative that runs contrary to our original capital policy. But it is a necessary step that will handle the immediate problem in an effective and relatively simple way.

We do not disagree with the position that previously-attained high capital ratios were intended for use in just such a current situation. Indeed, capital is supposed to absorb reductions in the value of a bank's assets. Any unyielding, rigid, required capital ratio would defeat the basic purpose of capital as a buffer. At the same time, we would not permit a bank that is in trouble to remove capital in the form of dividends or higher payments to owner-managers. We also intend to work toward changes in laws and regulations that would require more capital in better times and that would allow a bank to insulate itself better from the risk of local economic depressions through more effective diversification.

Risk-related deposit insurance

A second major new supervisory policy that we will implement upon approval by Congress is a risk-based deposit insurance programme, authorising us to charge additional fees to those banks requiring more than normal supervision. As the law now stands, the FDIC charges a flat fee based solely on total deposits, excluding deposits held overseas. No consideration is given to an institution's overall risk or the amount of resources required to supervise the bank. We believe that banks posing higher than normal risks should pay higher premiums. It is hoped that higher premiums will serve to restrain risk-taking and have an impact on management's choice of the appropriate level of risk. We think this approach is equitable and is consistent with the private sector's concept of insurance. The details of such a programme remain to be worked out, but we find little opposition to the concept of varying premiums by risk.

Public disclosure

It would be remiss not to mention a most important element of supervision – namely public disclosure. We continue to encourage banks to disclose fully all relevant information regarding their financial condition, insider transactions, and their future prospects. Adequate information is necessary for the orderly functioning of markets and for customers and investors exposed to risk. We have publicly encouraged large depositors as well as the investment community to obtain and analyse quarterly statements of condition and income as well as Uniform Bank Performance Reports. The latter reports summarise a bank's performance relative to comparable banks. Disclosure complements our supervisory efforts by allowing the market to participate in the discipline of banks. All banks are concerned about how the investment community and the public perceives them, especially since a downgrading of a bank's debt can have a major impact on its ability to raise funds in the marketplace. But much more needs to be done to ensure that all depository institutions, not just a few, are subject to consistent disclosure policies. At the same time, we must find a way to accommodate these proper user needs without imposing red tape on our many small institutions.

In conjunction with other federal bank regulators, the FDIC is considering requiring that each bank annually submit a short, simple statement setting forth its financial statements, required securities law disclosures and its business plans. We believe these disclosures could enhance the stock of valuable public information concerning banks.

Staffing needs

Finally, I must say a word about the most important supervisory initiative of all – the development and retention of a competent staff. Our ability to supervise banks effectively is dependent on our having a cadre of experienced and capable examiners. The FDIC has devoted millions of dollars over the years to improve the skills of our people. As banks continue to diversify into new areas we will have to develop specialised skills necessary to evaluate new risks. At the same time, we also have to maintain a competent core of generalists to pull all the pieces together. While the lure of public service attracts some bright, hardworking, and dedicated individuals, the complexity of tomorrow's environment will demand that regulators retain the best and brightest. We also have to use the tools of analysis and data processing to help the examiners be more productive. This, I have found, is no small challenge.

Summary

In sum, all of the initiatives I have discussed are designed to enhance the effectiveness of supervision and to strengthen the banking system. Banks are considered special, because of their role in the payments system. That is why they are insured. Some would even say they are over-insured. A deregulated environment gives management opportunities to fail. But because of deposit insurance, bank management is often not held as accountable for failure as the management of a non-bank competitor. That is why strong supervision is so important to us in this environment. As supervisors we must find ways to increase that accountability to bank's depositors and their public.

Conclusion

Times have really changed. Traditionally, prudential supervisors have tended first to be wary of innovation and then have tried to 'regulate it to the eyeballs.' However, in recent years supervisors have changed their tune. They have become the advocates of innovation. They realise that deregulation can enhance the safety and soundness of the system by granting financial intermediaries the flexibility they need to operate efficiently and to compete on equal terms. But enhanced supervision must go hand-in-hand with regulatory reform. Approached sensibly, broad-based deregulation in tandem with careful supervision will foster a stronger, more responsible, more competitive banking system. And that is in the best interests of the public.

Panel discussion

QUESTION:

Leslie Johnstone – Research student Manchester Universtity
Mr Wilkinson mentioned, if I understood him correctly, that he is expecting 60 per cent of the market deals to be in the hands of ten large firms within 5 years. He also possibly suggests that if in ten years' time it will be down to 5, in 15 years' time there will be the big two or even the big one and, if so, what are the implications for the market and for all players?

ANSWER:

Philip Wilkinson – National Westminster Bank
No, that is too extreme. What I was trying to say is that I think the major players are going to be capitalised better. Those that are capitalised at an appropriate, and that means a high, level, and who have developed the capability for dealing across the world, which is vital because it will be a global market, and who have put in the necessary investment – we have heard of the back office machinery that is also absolutely vital – will be limited to a few very major players. But I do not believe that in 15 years' time it will be as you perhaps suggest.

William Seidman – US Federal Deposit Insurance Corporation
If I could just comment on that from the American point of view. I certainly don't know what will happen here, but if you look at the economic growth in our country, the 20 million new jobs in the last ten years, tended to be all of the small players and, in fact, we have lost employment in our major industries and so the whole financing market has to accommodate those smaller kinds of institutions. While we see a centralisation, we also see a great regionalisation and a growth of the ability of some of the middle-sized institutions to do a very good job with that fast-growing segment of the market.

Philip Wilkinson
Although I was talking of the securities markets, you are quite right. In the UK, too, the creation of jobs is coming in the small business sector. But that is, I think, something quite different.

Rodney Galpin – Bank of England
There is one point which is relevant to this consideration of a global market and the internationalisation which is taking place. There are practitioners in the market who have to, to a large degree, put their trust in the regulators around the world to get it right. It seems to me that this level playing field argument is quite important and more important, possibly, in relation to the larger institutions than to the smaller specialised ones, who may find their own niche in the market. One should not underplay the problems which are involved in the international harmonisation of what is now an international market. It is very important, and from a banking supervision point of view, one ought at least to be able to persuade the regulators in the big countries in the world that, where they are introducing innovative techniques there should be, as far as you can get it, a standard approach to those in balance sheet terms. It is not going to be at all easy to develop that and it becomes even more difficult in an area of supervision where there is not already the international co-operation which has begun to be developed in banking.

QUESTION:

Philip Wilkinson
Mr Galpin, how are you getting along with the Japanese in this respect?

ANSWER:

Rodney Galpin
There have already been proposals from the Japanese in relation to off-balance sheet items, which is one measure of their willingness to adopt this harmonised approach. Certainly I think it is fair to say that within the group of ten countries one does not detect among the governors of the central banks there any lack of commitment towards the desire to harmonise. I find it very difficult to know the precise reaction when, as you find in Japan for example, the banking supervisor or the securities supervisor is not the Bank of Japan and, therefore, there is another hurdle to jump at home. But certainly, and Andrew Buxton mentioned the way in which the Japanese are opening up in Japan to houses from abroad, what I detect in my talks with Japanese bankers who want to come to London, is that they are going to be as good a pressure as any on their own regulators back home.

QUESTION:

Dr Catherine P. Smith – University of Stirling
Surely one of the things that we have got to recognise in the Bank of England regulation or financial institution regulation, wherever we are, is that any country's natural instinct is to put national profit before international equity. There will inevitably be one or two countries where it will be advantageous for an institution to operate, and this is going to be the major problem, surely, with the globalisation of financial institutions over the next 20 years as a result of dropping of barriers in some countries, improvements in technological capability and so on. What will be the impact on the regulators and on the types of regulation required as a result of that trend?

ANSWER:

Rodney Galpin
It would be foolish to seek to deny that aren't national interests always in play. The attraction of a financial centre is not necessarily just the regulation that is in place. There are a number of other factors which are also taken into account. Inadequate supervision and regulation seem to me to carry risks which can be quite damaging to the national interest. That sort of pressure is as important as any other in getting standards which are as uniform as they can be around the world, but it won't be easy.

Philip Wilkinson
It has already been mentioned but there is something that is really quite encouraging *vis-à-vis* the Japanese, who were particularly anxious to get into London – the security houses, Nomura and the others. The Government and the Bank of England exercised considerable bargaining power with the Japanese authorities and the sanctions that could be applied to the Japanese houses were relaxed once the Japanese authorities said they would do the same. In that respect there is the beginning of open competition but, like Mr Galpin, I agree that national profit motives, particularly when Japanese institutions work as a body, whether they are making cars or television sets, or even getting into financial business, sometimes become paramount.

Sir Kenneth Berrill – The Securities and Investments Board
I do not think it is true that the business would automatically go to the most lightly regulated place, because there are so many other reasons why you go to a particular place. There will be a concentration in the three various time zones. It is natural that the New York/Chicago axis should be the centre of the US time zone. It would be natural that Tokyo should be the centre in Japan, but it has not really been allowed to because it has been closed, so Hong Kong has been given a chance to expand. In Europe, London has in some ways a great many advantages, but not such tremendous advantages that risks of losing business to

other competing centres – Zurich, Frankfurt and so on – are small. But there is not really an opportunity to say 'well, shall we take it all to Andorra or elsewhere just because they have light regulation?' There are all sorts of other communications and legal arrangements and so on which count. So I think the battle will be between the credible alternatives in a given time zone – the stuff's not going to go down to Latin America you know, that's not going to work.

Another thing about internationalisation and round-the-clock markets, is that talking about ten or so major firms in the London market is counting every country. So the battle begins with four major Japanese houses, – and there have been four for quite a long time – as many Americans as you would like to count and clearly two major continental houses. So that after five or ten years the number of those ten firms which are likely to be British is a lot less. It is like sourcing motor cars: it is a world market. At least five of those ten would be overseas houses.

On the question of national interest, the Bill before Parliament that I have been concerned with gives me no discretion at all to distinguish on the origin of the person who is being authorised. It is colour-blind. The only relevant clause is the one which we are talking of, which is carefully reserved to the Secretary of State to make a decision on reciprocity grounds. He can do that, but when systems are set up, as far as I can see, they have to be set up with no reference to who the person is supplying, or to the background, in terms of country.

William Seidman
We in the United States have some experience with multiple regulators, since there at least four Federal regulators and 50 State regulators. So we have a similar problem of the lax areas and whether people will move to that area. We have found that the greatest danger is the inability to look at the whole institution when it is in several places and has several regulators responsible for the various parts, in that errors are more likely to drop between the chairs, or are purposely shoved there. As an old auditor myself I must say that more frauds occur between related parties, because related parties can shift assets around; and with the speed that you can do that around the world to-day, it will test the finest regulatory skills we have, simply to prevent the use of these various countries as a way to avoid detection of problems which may be present.

John Bullock – Deloitte Haskins & Sells
It seems to me that there is a parallel between this world-wide regulatory process and what happened with the auditing profession. There was a drive for consistent standards throughout the world not just because the regulatory bodies thought it was a good idea but also because the major multinational companies were themselves insisting on having more common standards in reporting and, surely, what we will see is the big houses themselves trying for consistent standards of approach. The whole process of this regulation can, in a lot of ways, be seen as a help and a lot of the players in the market, I would have thought, would welcome, a consistency of monitoring which makes life much

easier for them in terms of helping them manage their world-wide operations. If we see what has happened in the auditing profession around the world, that gradually you get consistency of standards, we could see the same pressures building up here.

QUESTION:

Paul Draper – University of Strathclyde
In the past we have regulated by institutions: by building societies and life assurance societies. It seems to me that we should be moving into a situation where we regulate by product, so that we regulate by mortgages. Anybody who wants to compete in the mortgage market should do so on equal terms. There again in long term savings, equity savings, anybody who provides equity savings plans ought to compete on the same terms whether they are a unit trust, investment trust or whatever. Can the panel comment on that?

ANSWER:

Sir Kenneth Berrill
That is the way it is likely to be. The grouping is broadly by product, if you like, and not by institution. It is the securities markets, the forward markets or the commodities markets, and the retail products. You are quite right. If an institution is involved in a range of products the problem is that it has got to register with more than one regulatory body.

QUESTION:

Paul Draper – University of Strathclyde
We do have building society regulations which can be quite separate, don't we?

ANSWER:

Sir Kenneth Berrill
Building society regulations won't be separate if they want to come into the investment business, no.

QUESTION:

Paul Draper – University of Strathclyde
Is it correct that mortgages are going to be given by banks and building societies and others, and are to be treated differently.

ANSWER:

Sir Kenneth Berrill
In so far as building societies wish to get into the life assurance linked ways of financing mortgages, they come on the financial services side of the house. The extent to which the building societies' operations like banks, will be in, as it were, the SIB area as distinct from the Registrar of Building Societies, depends on the extent to which building societies will be given a wide range or a narrow range of extra functions. It seems likely that even in the narrow range some of their business will be on the financial services side.

William Seidman
I would like to say that that is another stalemate in the United States at the moment. The Bush Commission has recommended that regulation shifts to functional regulation and that requires a lot of movement of turf and that turf movement is not accepted well by the Congress.

Rodney Galpin
I agree with Mr Draper that that is how we should be trying to do it, and as a banking supervisor I do not want, in any sense, to get on Sir Kenneth's territory in relation to his codes of conduct. The SIB or all the supervisors may have a problem of overlap in relation to capital adequacy. One has to find some convenient way of dealing with that or return filling to two different authorities who may have different views, and somehow you want to be able to reconcile those. If you can get to a situation when, for instance, one supervisor can be satisfied that the capital adequacy test which he would set is being met by the other supervisor, that may give you the possibility of reducing the overlap in supervision which might otherwise occur.

Sir Kenneth Berrill
The capital adequacy problems are not quite as bad as they might first seem, in that, for quite large areas of business, there is not a great deal of difficulty – the capital adequacy if you are an intermediary, the capital adequacy, if your are just managing people's money, etc. The capital adequacy problems come in the risk areas where you are taking positions, and taking positions mainly in the securities area. It is in the ISRO/Stock Exchange area, that the main issue of giving comparable rules of capital adequacy will match up with the banks' side on measuring risk exposures.

QUESTION:

Richard Dale
Where do the members of the panel think the pressure points may be in the next bear market?

ANSWER:

Philip Wilkinson
On the new market-makers – a very severe pressure point.

William Seidman
The United States, while a very prosperous nation, also has a depression in the mid-section of the country. So there is a little microcosm of what may happen in our banks and other institutions, and clearly the pressure on the banks is very large. Some of the problems of the freedom with which they have operated in this sort of general inclination of mankind to do things in excess from time to time, are showing up in those institutions, so I think you can clearly see that depository institutions are going to be one of the pressure points.

Sir Kenneth Berrill
Clearly, taking a risk position, and getting it wrong in a falling market is bad but, on the whole, many of the problems are connected with volume changes. If you have a bear market and the volume drops very very low and everybody's got overheads and costs running on like that, it depends how quickly they can get their 'survival kit' out and cut their overheads back if the volumes fall sharply. Some people think of the bear market as being only a question that prices have fallen; I think the effects of volume falling are equally worrying.

Professor Robert Jack – University of Glasgow/McGrigor Donald & Moncrieff
One of the casualties might be the SIB because who is going to pay for it when the volume is falling? I mean the staff might suddenly disappear like snow off a dyke. It is a serious problem because, in fact, unless you have the 'survival kit' in place and working effectively when the crunch comes, it is not going to serve a useful purpose: are petitioners going to be able to pay when they see their bottom line plunging into the red? It is a very real and serious problem, it seems to me, and the test will be like so many things in the bear market, like the liquidation I was talking about earlier.

Sir Kenneth Berrill
I have a lot of worries but that is not one of them. Just simply, if we are employing 100 people and the rest of the institutions are employing a million plus, I do not really think that our particular overhead is a serious one. Secondly, whether you like it or not, it is a levy and the only way to avoid it is to go bankrupt.

William Seidman
In that regard, the Federal Deposit Insurance Corporation currently has a net worth of approximately $18 billion. In its worst year, which was 1985, when we booked the loss for Continental Illinois, a bank that we now own and operate, we still added $1.4 billion to our surplus and that is giving a lot of confidence to the banking system at this particular time.

Sir Kenneth Berrill
I don't think I am allowed to build up so much in the good times but I will think about it.

John Bullock
Timing is crucial and the question should be more when is it coming, not what will be the result. From a service industry point of view I can only support what has been said on overheads. A business with highly fluctuating volumes has to realise that it is very dangerous to build up overheads on the basis of a high volume. When one is looking at supervision, surely you are looking at the extent to which the various players in the market are possibly over-extended in the likelihood of a downturn.

Rodney Galpin
I would only add that if Mr Buxton had said that Barclays were pulling out of retail banking, I might have been more fussed that I am.

QUESTION:

Professor Robert Jack
Could the crash of 1974, when property was the name of the game happen again, and will the subjects for discussion here contribute more to it happening than the previous regime? Securities are the name of the game now and what happens if the crash comes there?

ANSWER:

Philip Wilkinson
Generally, something like that probably will happen again, yes. I think you have to accept that the lessons learned in 1974 were taken to heart, at least for the first ten years, and then some strange things happened before some institutions pulled up short and said steady, steady.

QUESTION:

Dr Catherine P. Smith – University of Stirling
Can Sir Kenneth tell us who owns the SIB and is it for sale?

ANSWER:

Sir Kenneth Berrill
The SIB is a small company, limited by guarantee, but the Articles of Association were, not written by, but agreed with the Department of Trade and Industry and the Bank of England and they do not permit a take-over bid.